The
CONSTITUTION
of the
UNITED STATES

the text of this book is printed
on 100% recycled paper

The
CONSTITUTION
of the
UNITED STATES
With Case Summaries

Edited by

EDWARD CONRAD SMITH

BARNES & NOBLE BOOKS

A DIVISION OF HARPER & ROW, PUBLISHERS

New York, Evanston, San Francisco, London

First BARNES & NOBLE BOOKS edition published 1972.

LIBRARY OF CONGRESS CATALOG CARD NUMBER: 72–76888

STANDARD BOOK NUMBER: 06–460148–x

PREFACE

In 1936, Barnes & Noble published a small paperback book containing complete texts of the Constitution of the United States and the Declaration of Independence, with explanatory notes and charts by William R. Barnes. It was a time of unusual interest in the Constitution because of the apparent determination by a conservative majority of the Supreme Court to prevent important New Deal legislation from becoming effective. Interest in the Constitution has continued during later controversies over the proper scope of federal authority and interpretation of guarantees in the Bill of Rights and the Fourteenth Amendment. Various reprintings of this book have incorporated additional textual and explanatory material concerning the development of the written Constitution and its amendments.

The principal feature of this greatly enlarged edition is the inclusion of digests of cases which show how the meaning of the Constitution has been developed by judicial interpretation. In a sense this new material balances and completes the book. Only the most important cases have been summarized—those in which the Supreme Court departed by one or a few giant strides from accepted canons of interpretation and established new landmarks for the decision of future cases. The digests are highly concentrated and should be supplemented wherever possible by a reading of cases or of systematic treatises.

The author's thanks are due to Miss Nancy Cone, Editor of Barnes & Noble Books, who has had much to do with this edition from the inception of the idea through all the stages to its conclusion, and to Arnold J. Zurcher for permission to use some case summaries which he originally prepared for Smith and Zurcher, *Dictionary of American Politics,* Second Edition (New York: Barnes & Noble, 1968).

CONTENTS

Preface	v
THE ORIGINS OF THE CONSTITUTION	1
Revolution and Independence	2
State Constitutions	3
The Confederation of the States	4
The Movement for a New Constitution	6
The Convention of 1787	8
The Contest over Ratification	14
Changes in the Constitution by Amendment	16
DOCUMENTS	
Virginia Bill of Rights	21
Declaration of Independence	24
Articles of Confederation	28
Constitution of the United States	37
THE SUPREME COURT AND THE CONSTITUTION	59
SELECTED CASES	
Judicial Review	65
The Process of Amendment	66
Implied Powers	66
Supremacy of Federal Law	67
The Place of the States in the Nation	68
Federal Guarantees to States	68
Full Faith and Credit	69

Suffrage and Elections 70
Primary Elections 71
Legislative Districting 72
Legislative Privilege 73
Investigative Powers of Congress 73
The Taxing Power 74
The Spending Power 76
Scope of the Commerce Power 77
Navigation 78
Railroad Rates and Services 78
State Police Powers over Interstate Commerce 79
The Original Package Doctrine 80
Federal Regulation of Business 81
Federal Regulation of Insurance 82
Federal Regulation of Agriculture 83
Federal Legislation Concerning Labor 83
Borrowing and Currency 84
War Powers 86
Government of Territories and Dependencies 87
Delegation of Power 88
Bill of Attainder 89
Obligation of a Contract 89
The Presidency 90
The Removal Power 92
The President and Foreign Affairs 92
Treaties and Executive Agreements 93
The President as Commander in Chief 95
The Pardoning Power 96
Judicial Organization 97
Jurisdiction of the Federal Courts 97
Interstate Controversies 99
Diversity of Citizenship 100
The Bill of Rights 100
Freedom of Speech 101

Symbolic Speech   104
Freedom of Speech and Assembly   104
Freedom of the Press   105
Obscenity   106
Broadcasting   107
Freedom of Religion   107
Unreasonable Searches and Seizures   110
Self-Incrimination   111
Double Jeopardy   113
Trial by Jury   114
Cruel and Unusual Punishment   116
Right of Counsel   116
Thirteenth Amendment   118
Fourteenth Amendment: Citizenship   118
Privileges and Immunities of Citizens   120
Due Process under the Fourteenth Amendment   120
State Labor Legislation   121
Equal Protection of the Laws   123
Equal Protection in Education   124
QUALIFICATIONS AND POWERS OF FEDERAL OFFICERS   127
CHARTS AND TABLES
Government of the United States   130
Entrance of States into Union   131
Territories and Dependencies   132
Presidents of the United States   133
Judicial Organization of the United States   135
Supreme Court Justices since 1789   137
Selected References   140
Index Guide to the Constitution   143
Alphabetical Index of Cases   145

THE ORIGINS
OF THE CONSTITUTION

The Constitution of 1787 was the product of seven centuries of development in England and America. Magna Charta (1215) is as much the heritage of Americans as of Englishmen. So is the common law which limited the authority of the King's ministers as well as governed the King's subjects. The rights and privileges of Parliament were claimed by colonial legislatures against royal governors. From experience in living under charters in some of the colonies, Americans learned the value of written documents which explicitly stated the rights of the people and the government's powers. They were constantly trying to adapt English institutions to the conditions of a new continent and a relatively classless society.

The breach between England and the Americans resulted from their diametrically opposed ideas as to the proper political relationship of the colonies to the mother country. King George III, his ministers, and majorities in Parliament regarded the colonies as subordinate to England. The Americans regarded each colony as a coequal part of the King's dominions and, as such, entitled to self-government and exemption from parliamentary taxation and legislation, and administrative interference. They sought redress of grievances by protests, petitions, nonimportation agreements, and, at last, by resorting to arms.

In May, 1775, three weeks after the Revolutionary War began at Lexington and Concord, the Second Continental Congress met at Philadelphia. It was a revolutionary body deriving its authority from other revolutionary bodies. Its members were delegates of patriotic organizations in each of the colonies sent to concert measures for the common defense. Congress assumed many of the powers of government; it created an army and navy, appointed officers, borrowed money, issued paper currency, and sought help from Europe. It adopted the

1

Declaration of Independence, recommended the creation of state constitutions, and drew up the Articles of Confederation, all highly important in American constitutional development.

REVOLUTION AND INDEPENDENCE

Though a few radical leaders advocated independence from the beginning, most Americans hoped for eventual reconciliation with Great Britain. The Congress, on July 6, 1775, issued a lengthy "Declaration of the Causes and Necessity of Taking up Arms," detailing American grievances but explicitly denying an intention to separate from Great Britain and establish independent states. King George replied by proclaiming a state of rebellion in the colonies, and Parliament dutifully passed an act cutting off colonial trade. Moderate leaders now became convinced that independence was the only alternative to submission. Thomas Paine's emotion-charged pamphlet, *Common Sense,* was heavily circulated throughout the colonies and converted thousands of ordinary Americans to the cause of independence. On June 6, 1776, Richard Henry Lee of Virginia proposed the following to the Continental Congress:

> *Resolved,* That these United Colonies are, and of right ought to be, free and independent States, that they are absolved from all allegiance to the British Crown, and that all political connection between them and the State of Great Britain is, and ought to be totally dissolved.

Drafting the Declaration. On June 10 Congress appointed its five most able members—John Adams, Benjamin Franklin, Thomas Jefferson, Robert R. Livingston, and Roger Sherman—as a committee to draft the Declaration. Jefferson was chief author of the draft that was submitted to Congress on June 23. Congress made two or three changes and voted independence on July 2. On July 4 the engrossed copy was signed by John Hancock, President of the Congress. All but one of the other signatures were appended on August 2.

Contents of the Declaration. The underlying philosophy of the Declaration of Independence was derived from John Locke's second treatise *On Civil Government* (1690), which had been written with the avowed purpose of justifying the English Revolution of 1688. According to Locke, men had once lived unrelated lives in a state of nature.

At a certain stage of development they entered into a social contract with one another, thereby creating both a society and a government. By the terms of the contract each individual surrendered part of his natural rights, and in return received protection and other advantages of organized government. The acts of government must be in accordance with moral principles, what is right or wrong being determined by the will of the majority. If a government seriously threatens the interests of society, the people may pull it down and substitute another government for it. Jefferson omitted a specific reference to the imaginary state of nature and social contract, and asserted that the natural equality of men and their natural rights are "self-evident."

The main body of the Declaration contains twenty-six indictments against the King and Parliament for usurpations and tyrannical acts, such as "abolishing our most valuable laws," and "waging war against us." For these reasons, in the name of the people, the United Colonies were declared free and independent states with all the powers rightfully belonging to sovereign states.

Effects of the Declaration. The Declaration of Independence was a powerful stimulus to the patriot cause. It was both a brilliant justification for resort to arms and an implied promise that American successor governments would be founded on the will of the people. Though it did not immediately result in the emancipation of slaves or in universal suffrage, advocates of both abolition of slavery and suffrage extension in later generations effectively used the equalitarian principles of the Declaration to advance their causes. In our own day it is a prod to the consciences of the American people to improve the conditions of minority groups.

STATE CONSTITUTIONS

Beginning in 1776, revolutionary assemblies in most states formulated written constitutions, using colonial charters as models. All of them had certain common features.

Popular Sovereignty. The people were everywhere declared to be the source of governmental authority. In the words of the Georgia constitution of 1777: "We, therefore, the representatives of the people, from whom all power originates and for whose benefit all government is intended, by virtue of the power delegated to us, do ordain . . . that the following rules and regulations be adopted for the future government of this state." The Massachusetts constitution of 1780 expressed the same idea in the form of an original social contract: "The whole people covenants with each citizen, and each citizen with the whole people that all shall be governed by certain laws for the common good."

Eclipse of the Executive. Executive power in the states entered an eclipse that lasted until the adoption of the Constitution of the United States. The first constitution of Pennsylvania did not provide for a governor. In ten states the governor's term was only one year and his administrative powers were few. Only New York gave the governor sufficient power and a long enough term (three years) to make him truly the head of the executive branch.

Legislative Supremacy. In a majority of the states the legislature elected the governor, judges, and other officers and determined the policies of government. It possessed lawmaking, financial, and supervisory powers granted in general terms. As the successor of Parliament, the legislature was considered to hold general residual authority in the government and therefore could exercise any power not granted to another authority. Except in Pennsylvania and Georgia, the legislature was composed of two houses. In most states members were chosen by voters who were required to own a considerable amount of property.

Limited Government. The most remarkable document issued by any state in this period was the Bill of Rights which was prefixed to the Virginia constitution of 1776. The first fifteen articles were written by George Mason. The sixteenth article, on religious freedom, was written by Patrick Henry. This document states the principles on which all parts of the government, including the legislature, should be conducted. It incorporated guarantees to protect the liberties of the individual. It was influential in the writing of later constitutions both in the United States and in Europe.

THE CONFEDERATION OF THE STATES

The same Virginia resolution that proposed independence called upon Congress to prepare a plan for confederation of the states. On July 12, 1776, debate began on a draft written by John Dickinson, and continued at intervals whenever time could be spared from urgent military matters. It soon became apparent that selfish concerns of the states outweighed considerations of national interest. States with claims to western lands refused to grant Congress power to settle boundary disputes. The small states insisted on amendments to secure their sovereignty. The large states tried (in vain) to apportion voting strength in Congress according to population or the amount that each state contributed to the common fund. The Southern states insisted that expenses of the Confederation should be apportioned according to the value of land in private hands rather than according to total population including slaves. It was not until November 1, 1777, that Congress submitted the Articles to the states for ratification.

Most of the states ratified fairly promptly, but Maryland, expressing fears for her future among powerful neighbors, held out until other states agreed to cede their western lands to the United States. The Articles became effective on March 1, 1781.

Structure of the Confederation. The Articles variously describe the new arrangement as a "confederacy," as a "firm league of friendship," and as a "perpetual Union." It was less a government than an agency for cooperation among state governments. Each state retained its sovereignty, freedom, and independence. The Articles could be amended only with the unanimous approval of the state legislatures. There was no provision for an executive or a permanent judiciary. The chief organ of government was a Congress composed of delegations of from two to seven persons, chosen annually, from each state. Each delegation was paid by the state from which it came, and was subject to recall. Each delegation was entitled to cast one vote, and the approval of nine states was required for any important action. The Articles contained numerous provisions for securing cooperation among the states, including a full-faith-and-credit clause and a privileges-and-immunities clause. Several limitations on state action that were expressed in Article VI were later carried over into the Constitution of the United States; and so were many of the powers granted to Congress in Article IX. The fatal defects of the Articles were in their omissions. They did not provide for a vigorous executive. They did not grant to Congress control over commerce between the states and with foreign countries. Worst of all, they failed to give Congress an independent means of raising revenue by taxation. It could only apportion needed amounts as "requisitions" upon the states, which were then supposed to levy appropriate taxes and remit the proceeds. The authority of Congress could not be directly exerted upon individuals.

The Confederation Period. Unsettled economic conditions at the close of the Revolution severely tested both the state governments and the Congress. In some states the legislatures felt compelled to yield to the demands of debtors and issue excessive quantities of paper money or enact "stay laws," or moratoria, postponing the dates when debtors were legally obliged to pay their creditors. In violation of the terms of the Articles, some states imposed tariffs or other trade barriers preventing the free flow of commerce from other states. In varying degrees states failed in their financial obligations to the Confederation. Of a total of $10,000,000 requisitioned by Congress, only $1,500,000 was actually paid; one state paid nothing at all. Largely because of Congress's inability to meet interest payments when due, the public debt increased after the close of the Revolution. The government of the Confederation was maintaining only a small army, 750 officers and men, for the defense of the United States against Indians and other potential enemies. By the Ordinances of 1785 and 1787, Congress established fundamental and durable policies for the survey of public lands and the government of territories, but was unable to promote much settlement in the Northwest Territory. Though the ablest leaders of the country were engaged in diplomacy, they were singularly unsuccessful in negotiating commercial treaties, in part because foreign nations feared that the states would not fulfill the treaty obligations of the United States.

Failure of the Amending Process. In 1781 Congress proposed an amendment to the Articles which would have enabled it to levy a duty of five per cent on all imported goods. All the states ratified the amendment except Rhode Island. A second amendment designed to meet Rhode Island's objections was ratified by twelve states, but this time it was New York that refused to give its approval despite the warning of Congress that without revenues the Confederation would disintegrate. Both Rhode Island and New York possessed fine harbors which served as ports of entry for the trade of nearby states, and both were unwilling to concede any considerable part of the tariff duties for the common good. The attitude of the dominant political groups in these states made it plain that, if the Union were to be strengthened, it must be done by some means other than the cumbrous procedure required by the Articles.

THE MOVEMENT FOR A NEW CONSTITUTION

A number of groups combined in an effort to create the Constitution of the United States. Among the most important were former officers of the Continental Army and former members of Congress who, in the course of their service, had developed national loyalties; leaders from the large states of Virginia, Pennsylvania, and Massachusetts who believed that the ability of one state to veto progress endangered the future of all the states; leaders from the small states of Connecticut, New Jersey, and Delaware who desired relief from the commercial restrictions of New York and Pennsylvania; Georgians who wanted national help against a threatened Indian war; and merchants and shipowners in all the states. The most active leaders of the movement were Alexander Hamilton of New York who, as military secretary to Washington, had observed the weakness and incapacity of Congress; and James Madison, an ardent nationalist, associate of Jefferson, and opponent of Patrick Henry in Virginia politics.

The Call for the Convention. In 1785 commissioners from Virginia and Maryland settled amicably many disputed points concerning boundaries, navigation in the Chesapeake Bay, and tariff duties. When the Maryland commissioners proposed a larger conference to include Delaware and Pennsylvania, the Virginia legislature seized the opportunity to call a meeting of delegates from all the states at Annapolis in September, 1786. Nine states responded by appointing delegates, but only five states were represented when the conference met. Those present adopted a strongly worded report, supposed to have been written by Hamilton, stressing the deficiencies in the existing government of the United States and calling a convention of all the states to meet in Philadelphia, May 14, 1787, for the purpose of "digesting a Plan" for remedying the defects of the Articles of Confederation. After several states had chosen delegates, Congress issued a formal call for a convention "for the sole and express purpose of revising the Articles of Confederation."

The Selection of Delegates. The Virginia legislature selected an able delegation including Washington, who was prevailed upon to come out of retirement and throw the weight of his influence in favor of the movement, James Madison, George Mason, and Governor Edmund Randolph. The Pennsylvania delegation was the largest, including Franklin, whose reputation was second only to that of Washington; James Wilson, who had consistently expressed the belief that the Americans were one people; and Gouverneur Morris, a brilliant New Yorker temporarily residing in Philadelphia. The New York legislature designated Hamilton but took care to send with him John Lansing and Robert Yates, members of the dominant antifederalist party in the state. The New Hampshire legislature chose delegates but neglected to provide for their expenses; they arrived in late July—after Lansing and Yates of the New York delegation had withdrawn from the convention. Rhode Island alone appointed no delegates, and was unrepresented throughout the deliberations. Other delegates of outstanding abilities were Rufus King and Elbridge Gerry of Massachusetts, Roger Sherman and William Samuel Johnson of Connecticut, and John Rutledge and the two Pinckneys of South Carolina.

Of the fifty-five delegates who attended the convention, thirty-nine had served in Congress, and all were experienced in the politics of their states. A large number of the delegates were young men in their early thirties; the average age was about forty-three. Among those who did not attend the convention were Jefferson and John Adams who were abroad as ministers to France and Great Britain respectively. Patrick Henry and a number of other leaders whose interests were primarily in state politics declined to serve.

THE CONVENTION OF 1787

Only the Virginia and Pennsylvania delegations were in Philadelphia at the appointed time, and it was not until May 25 that the Convention could be organized for business. The delegates unanimously elected Washington as presiding officer. Rules of procedure provided that each state delegation should have one vote. The delegates agreed to keep their deliberations absolutely secret, an action that is partly responsible for the theory—now generally discredited—that they engaged in an undemocratic conspiracy to undo the work of the Revolution. The rule of secrecy enabled the members to express opinions freely and without reserve, to advance tentative proposals, to reconsider decisions without being publicly ridiculed for inconsistency, to compromise, and to concede points in return for intangible advantages. They determined to prepare a comprehensive document and be judged on their work as a whole.

Records of the Convention. Madison, sensing the historical importance of the Convention, obtained its permission to take copious notes on the debates. Other members sometimes helped by giving him copies or outlines of their remarks. Madison's notes, which became available to the public only after his death in 1836, constitute practically the only dependable source of information concerning the debates. In some matters they were supplemented by the recollections of other delegates written after the Convention had adjourned.

The Virginia Plan. After their arrival in Philadelphia, the Virginia delegation drafted a series of resolutions to serve, instead of the Articles of Confederation, as a basis for the discussions. The plan provided for the supremacy of the legislative branch, a national executive, and a system of national courts. The legislature should consist of two houses, one of which should be elected by popular vote, and the other selected by the first house from persons nominated by the state legislatures. A state's voting strength in each house should be in proportion to the amounts contributed by the state or to the number of its free inhabitants. The legislature should have power to enact laws in all cases to which the separate states were incompetent; to disallow state laws contravening the constitution; to call forth the forces of the Union against any recalcitrant state; and to elect the national executive and the judges of national courts.

The delegates debated the Virginia plan for two weeks, making a number of changes. It was agreed that representatives in the lower house should be apportioned according to population, and also—by a margin of one vote—that the same apportionment apply to the second house. The delegation from New Jersey requested an adjournment in order to prepare a different plan.

The New Jersey Plan. On June 15 William Paterson of the New Jersey delegation introduced resolutions that the Convention should confine itself to proposing amendments to the Articles of Confederation as Congress had specified. It suggested that Congress should be granted power to levy duties on foreign goods imported into the United States, to impose a stamp tax on documents, and to regulate the collection of both. If additional revenue was needed, Congress could not only requisition the states, but direct the collection of taxes in noncomplying states. Congress should have power to regulate foreign and interstate commerce. All laws of Congress and all treaties made under the authority of the United States should be the supreme law of the respective states. There was to be a plural executive chosen by Congress, with general authority to execute federal acts, appoint federal officers, and direct all military operations. There was to be a supreme court appointed by the executive with jurisdiction on appeal over cases arising from the construction of treaties, the acts for the regulation of trade, and the collection of revenue.

If the New Jersey plan had been formulated before the Convention met, it would have been satisfactory to all but the most advanced nationalists. As it was, it received the support of New York and Delaware only. But it became obvious that many of the proposals of the

Virginia plan, in particular the apportionment of the upper house according to population, would have to be reconsidered if the support of the small states was to be won.

The Great Compromise. At this point the lines between the large and small states became tightly drawn, and there was talk of breaking up the Convention. The delegates from large states refused to yield on the principle of representation in proportion to population; the small states feared to enter a union completely dominated by the large states. Besides, they argued, the people would never accept a constitution that did not preserve the principle of state equality. After three weeks of recriminations, the delegates agreed to the Great (sometimes called the Connecticut) Compromise: the lower house should be chosen according to population and should have the sole authority to originate revenue bills; and each state would have an equal vote in the upper house.

Compromise of Sectional Interests. Northern commercial interests were anxious for Congress to have power to regulate commerce, and delegates had willingly conceded to the South that no export duties could be levied. In addition to free exportation of their staple crops, the Southerners demanded that Congress be denied power in interfere with the slave trade. The compromise finally arrived at provided, in return for the commerce power, that the slave trade might continue until 1808 with a duty of not more than $10 for each slave imported.

The formula for counting three-fifths of the slaves in apportioning representatives and direct taxes was carried over from one of the unsuccessful amendments previously proposed by Congress.

The Powers of Congress. One by one the broad general grants of power in the Virginia plan were found to be impractical. To disallow state laws would cause resentment, and to use military force was practically equivalent to making war on a state. The delegates decided to enumerate the specific powers which Congress might exercise. The Committee on Detail compiled a list, taking most of the powers—some of them verbatim—from the Articles of Confederation; and others from various state constitutions. From this list the Convention chose many provisions to be included in the Constitution. The taxing power was granted in broad terms, practically unrestrained except as to direct taxes. The necessary-and-proper clause at the end of the enumerated powers gave Congress a choice of means in carrying out the powers of the federal government.

The Executive Article. Nothing gave the Convention so much trouble as the problem of how to create an executive with adequate powers and yet with requisite responsibility to the people. The delegates debated the merits of a plural, as against a single, executive, and considered tenure for life and for seven years without re-eligibility before settling on a four-year term with re-eligibility. In provisions borrowed from the constitution of New York, the Convention created a strong executive; but they made him subject to impeachment and trial by the houses of Congress. As to the method of choosing the President, the Convention discarded legislative election because it would make the President subservient to Congress; and popular election, because it would give excessive influence to the large states. The final solution was the electoral college which was heavily weighted in favor of the small states. The least populous state would have three electors, and a state with ten times as many people would only have four times as many electors. If no candidate received a majority of the electoral college vote, the House of Representatives, voting by states and with each state having one vote, would select from among the five highest candidates. It was expected that Washington would be the first President and would serve as long as he cared to. After that, it was thought the electoral vote would be scattered among celebrities in different states, and the election would be thrown into the House where the small states, being in the majority, would, in fact, choose the President.

The Judiciary Article. The Convention early agreed that there should be a supreme court and that all federal judges should have tenure during good behavior. Sharp differences of opinion arose over whether to create a separate system of lower federal courts or to provide for the trial of federal cases in existing state courts. Without settling the issue, the Convention got it out of the way by providing that Congress might create inferior federal courts. But the Supreme Court was given original jurisdiction to decide cases involving foreign diplomatic and consular officers and disputes between states. Federal judges were to be appointed by the President with the consent of the Senate.

The Supremacy Clause. In Article VI, a provision which had first appeared in the New Jersey plan declared that the Constitution and all laws made in accordance with it, and all treaties, past and future, should be the supreme law of the land. All state judges were bound to uphold the supremacy of valid federal laws and treaties, even if they were in conflict with state constitutions or state laws. Another clause designed to strengthen the Union required all state legislative, executive and judicial officers to take an oath to support the Constitution of the United States.

The Position of States under the Constitution. The federal government was required to guarantee to each state a republican form of government, and to protect it from invasion, and, at its request, from domestic violence. No state, without its own consent, could be divided, or joined with another state, or be deprived of its equal vote in the Senate. Nothing was said about state sovereignty. States were forbidden to coin money, issue paper money, make anything but gold and silver coin a legal tender in payment of debts, pass any law impairing the obligation of contracts, levy taxes on imports or exports, or, without the consent of Congress, enter into a compact with another state. These prohibitions summed up the criticisms of the financial and business community against measures passed by several state legislatures during the confederation period. In order to promote harmonious relations with each other, states were required to give full faith and credit to acts and records of other states, to treat citizens of other states like their own citizens, and to return fugitives from justice and runaway slaves to the states from which they had fled.

Democratic Basis of the Constitution. The preamble of the Articles of Confederation had named all the states in order from north to south. How was the Convention to enumerate the participating states without knowing which would ratify? In a brilliant flash of inspiration, the Convention began with the words, "We the People of the United States . . . do ordain and establish this Constitution. . . ."

The Method of Ratification. The members apparently believed that ratification by state conventions specially elected by the people for the purpose was more democratic than ratification by state legislatures. Besides, as some delegates pointed out, the legislatures would be prejudiced against an instrument of government that would reduce their own powers. In view of the continued stubbornness of New York and Rhode Island, the Convention abandoned all thought of requiring ratification by every state. Allowing for some antifederalist opinion known to exist elsewhere, it voted that the Constitution should go into effect as soon as nine states had ratified. (Apparently non-ratifying states were to be left to their own resources.)

The Amending Procedure. The delegates were keenly aware that flaws in the Constitution might appear after it came into operation, and they were determined not to carry over the disastrous amending procedure of the Articles. At first they voted that Congress should call a convention to propose amendments at the request of two-thirds of the states. To further liberalize the amending procedure they agreed, toward the end of the session, that two-thirds of both houses of Congress might also propose amendments. No matter which way they were proposed, amendments must be ratified either by the legislatures or by conventions in three-fourths of the states.

Guarantees of Rights. As finally agreed to, the Constitution contained several important guarantees of private rights: the privilege of habeas corpus and the prohibitions of bills of attainder and ex post facto laws in Article I, section 9; trial by jury and limitations on trials for treason in Article III; and a prohibition of religious tests for officers in Article VI. Opinions were expressed that a declaration of other rights would be superfluous because either they would not be endangered by federal authorities or would be covered by the common law. Late in the session George Mason and Elbridge Gerry proposed the appointment of a committee to draft a bill of rights; the motion failed by a tie vote.

The End of the Session. The provisions already voted were arranged in logical order by a committee on style. Gouverneur Morris is credited with having written the final draft. Of the fifty-five members who attended the sessions at some time, many had gone home. Thirty-nine signed the Constitution; Gerry, Mason, and Randolph for various reasons refused to sign. On September 17, the Convention adjourned, after having been in practically continuous session for nearly four months.

Political Theory of the Constitution. Madison and others had studied the history of previous federations, but fortunately had formulated no hard and fast theories on the subject. Their attitude was pragmatic. Every provision which they wrote into the Constitution was based on experience in the states, or the colonies, or the mother country. The assignment of power to the federal government was determined by what was needful and what might be acceptable to the state conventions. For theoretical inspiration they leaned heavily on Locke and on Montesquieu's *Spirit of the Laws*. Both writers had insisted on the need for a separation of powers in order to prevent tyranny; in Montesquieu's view even the representatives of the people in the legislature could not be trusted with unlimited power. So they incorporated the power of each branch in a separate article and then devised various checks and balances to compel cooperation among legislative, executive, and judicial branches. There was no mention of a state of nature or an original contract, but by basing the Constitution on the will of the people—as in the preamble and the ratification article —the Convention suggested to persons familiar with Locke's theories a latter-day social contract.

THE CONTEST OVER RATIFICATION

The Convention sent copies of the Constitution to Congress which transmitted them, without comment, to the states. More or less promptly (except in Rhode Island) the legislatures arranged for the selection of delegates to conventions. In the contest over ratification, the federalists, though a minority, had the advantage of unity, initiative, and a novel and interesting proposal. The opposition was divided, overconfident, and badly led.

Discussions in the Press. The text of the Constitution and arguments for and against its adoption occupied much of the space in all American newspapers during the ensuing months. The most noteworthy series of articles in favor of the Constitution was written by Hamilton, Madison, and John Jay for New York newspapers. Out of the terms of the Constitution, they constructed a theory of maximum liberty and governmental effectiveness through federalism; and on theoretical and practical grounds met the objections of the antifederalists. *The Federalist* papers (as the collected articles were later called) remain the best theoretical justification of the American federal system.

The best statement of the antifederalist position was made in a series of "Letters of the Federal Farmer" by Richard Henry Lee. He characterized the new system of government as partly federal but "calculated ultimately to make the states one consolidated government." He warned that adoption of the Constitution would be a fatal error because the government created under it might abolish the laws, customs, and constitutions already in existence in America. He thought the proposed House of Representatives would not be sufficiently responsive to the wishes of the people; and there was no bill of rights to protect individual liberties. He insisted that the Constitution be amended before, and not after, its adoption by the state conventions. Other antifederalists, taking a narrow legalistic approach, argued that the Convention had abused its authority, since it had been called only to propose amendments to the Articles of Confederation. They demanded to know by what authority the Convention had used the phrase, "We the People . . . ," since everyone knew that states were the parties to the compact that had created the Articles of Confederation. On practical grounds some antifederalists asserted that a federal government could not effectively exert power over so large a territory as the United States; others that its capital would become, as London had been, a center of concentrated power. Nearly every clause in the proposed constitution was subjected to adverse criticism.

Ratification of the Constitution. By mid-January, 1788, five state conventions had ratified—Delaware, New Jersey, and Georgia unanimously, and Connecticut and Pennsylvania by votes of two or three to one. Maryland approved on April 28 and South Carolina on May 23, by overwhelming majorities. Serious trouble was encountered in all other states. When the Massachusetts convention had met in January, preliminary votes showed that a majority of the delegates was opposed to the Constitution; they were led by Gerry, Samuel Adams, and John Hancock. After heated discussion, the opposition weakened, and Massachusetts ratified on February 6. In New Hampshire the federalists avoided defeat in January by procuring a long adjournment. After a bitter struggle, they won out on June 21, when New Hampshire became the ninth state to ratify. Four days later, the Virginia federalists under the leadership of Madison and John Marshall overcame an early disadvantage, despite the efforts of George Mason, Patrick Henry, and Richard Henry Lee. In New York the antifederalists at first had an advantage of two to one; but when the practical issue became whether to enter the Union or stay out, the convention ratified by a majority of three votes, July 26, 1788. The new government began with eleven states in the Union on April 30, 1789. North Carolina entered the Union the following November and Rhode Island more than a year later.

In the state conventions the principal strength of the federalists came from representatives of ship-owners, merchants, and handicraftsmen in the towns near the Atlantic coast, and of frontiersmen. These groups were apparently convinced of the need for more adequate foreign and military policies and an end to interstate trade barriers. Opposition to the Constitution was strongest among the people in upcountry agricultural areas where the principal needs were better roads and courthouse services, both of which state and local governments could supply. In varying degrees, antifederalist attitudes were determined by alignments in state and local politics, vague fears of a federal colossus, and the conviction, held especially in New York and Rhode Island, that the establishment of the new federal government would mean increased state and federal taxes on land and other property. In the debates over ratification, the most criticized feature of the Constitution was the lack of a bill of rights. The federalists promised that a bill of rights would be added later through the amendment process. They were not obliged to yield on any other point, but consistently gained support as the discussions in state conventions proceeded.

CHANGES IN THE CONSTITUTION BY AMENDMENT

In accordance with federalist promises, Madison, on June 8, 1789, introduced a number of proposed amendments in the House of Representatives. He intended them to be inserted at appropriate places in the text of the Constitution, but Roger Sherman persuaded Congress to add them at the end, so that each amendment would stand or fall on its own merits when submitted to state authorities for ratification. Congress decided that the President's signature to a proposed amendment is not required. These precedents and later Supreme Court decisions have governed the amending process. On no occasion have two-thirds of the states asked Congress to call a constitutional convention. Congress has proposed all amendments, determined their exact phraseology, and sometimes fixed a time limit of seven years within which the amendment must be accepted or considered rejected. With the exception of the Twenty-first Amendment, ratification has been by state legislatures. Once a legislature has ratified, neither it nor the voters of the state in a referendum may rescind the ratification. But ratification may occur by the same or a later legislature after previous failures to ratify. The Twenty-first Amendment was referred to state conventions in order to obtain the opinion of bodies especially chosen for the purpose of determining the amendment's subject, the future of national prohibition.

The Bill of Rights. The first ten amendments are called the Bill of Rights. Their contents are derived from English and colonial experience and from the vigorous American political thinking of the Revolutionary and Confederation periods, most lately expressed in the debates and resolutions of the state conventions which ratified the Constitution.

The First Amendment prohibits the establishment of a state-supported church, requires the separation of church and state, and guarantees freedom of worship, of speech and the press, and the rights of peaceable assembly and petition. The Supreme Court has shown a disposition to regard these rights of belief and expression as more fundamental than other parts of the Constitution. Indeed, a few justices have considered them as absolute freedoms. In periods of war or public fear of subversion, however, the Court has approved of some limitations upon them.

The Second and Third Amendments reflect the framers' fears of a standing army and of soldiers billeted in private households and the tendency of eighteenth-century Americans to rely on citizen soldiers for defense.

The Fourth to the Eighth Amendments are concerned with the protection of life, liberty, and property. Most of their detailed provisions are designed to protect citizens from improper conduct on the part of officers engaged in the enforcement of criminal law and to secure fair play in all procedures from the collection of evidence, arrest, and indictment to the final disposition of the case in a court of law. They have been held to prohibit official searches of all kinds without a warrant; wiretapping of private conversations whether in homes or public telephone booths; the use of illegally obtained evidence in the courtroom; confessions obtained by coercion or trickery; the denial of reasonable bail; double jeopardy; unduly delayed trials, trials without indictments, or trials at places far from the scene of the crime, or by juries from which members of the accused's race have been systematically excluded; and excessive or cruel punishments after conviction. An accused person is entitled to be informed of the charges against him, to confront his accusers in open court, and to have the court's help in compelling the attendance of witnesses who may testify on his behalf. He must be able to consult privately with his attorneys at all stages of the proceedings, and his attorneys must be allowed sufficient time to prepare his defense. If he is indigent, the court must provide counsel to defend him. The requirement of due process of law (equivalent to the English "law of the land") governs the interpretation of these and other matters, including the judge's fairness in conducting the trial and instructing the jury. The due-process clause also protects property rights against impairment by legislation in excess of Congress's powers, as well as from unfair acts and procedures by executive and administrative officers, quasi-legislative commissions, and courts of law.

The Ninth Amendment was probably intended to reassure the public that the enumeration of certain rights did not exclude the operation of the common law in maintaining others.

The Tenth Amendment was intended to limit centralizing tendencies in government. When it was being discussed in Congress, antifederalists made a determined but unsuccessful effort to confine the federal government to expressly granted powers and to reserve all others to the states or to the people thereof. As adopted without the word "thereof," the amendment leaves intact the principle of implied powers and acknowledges the existence of undefined powers belonging to the people of the whole country.

Later Amendments. The Eleventh Amendment prevents any person from suing a state in the federal courts. It was adopted after the Supreme Court took jurisdiction over a case (*Chisholm* v. *Georgia*), initiated under provisions of Article III, section 2, by a citizen of South Carolina.

The Twelfth Amendment adjusted the Constitution to the rise of national parties which the framers had not anticipated. In the election of 1800, all the Republican presidential electors having two votes for President cast one vote for Jefferson and one for Burr, the party's nominees for President and Vice President respectively. Since no one had a majority, the election devolved upon the House of Representatives. Before Jefferson was finally chosen, there was much unsavory maneuvering to elect Burr as President. To prevent a similar situation from recurring, the Twelfth Amendment gave each elector, instead of two votes for President, one vote for President and one vote for Vice President, to be cast on separate ballots.

The Thirteenth Amendment confirmed Lincoln's Emancipation Proclamation and freed all slaves (mostly those in border states) who had not been included in the Proclamation. The phrase "involuntary servitude" forbids peonage or forced labor under contract.

The Fourteenth Amendment resulted from the rejection of Southern doctrines of state sovereignty and secession. It made federal citizenship paramount, thus overriding the Supreme Court's strained construction of the Constitution (*Dred Scott* v. *Sandford,* 1857) which made citizenship by birth dependent on state law. By the due-process and equal-protection clauses it sought to safeguard the civil liberties of newly freed Negroes and others from state impairment. For many years the Supreme Court applied the due-process clause mainly to protect business interests against state regulatory legislation. But in a long series of cases beginning with *Gitlow* v. *New York* (1925), the Court gradually expanded its definition of due process so as to include most of the guarantees of personal liberties in the Federal Bill of Rights and has protected them from state impairment. A similar development occurred with respect to the equal-protection clause. In *Plessy* v. *Ferguson* (1896) the Court was satisfied that "separate but equal" public facilities met the requirement. In later cases, of which *Brown* v. *Board of Education of Topeka* (1954) is most significant, the Court held that the mere fact of segregation under state authority is inherently unequal.

The Fifteenth Amendment forbids denial of suffrage because of race, color, or previous condition of servitude; but several Southern states found other means, such as failure to pay a poll tax or pass an unfairly administered literacy tests, which until recently were effective bars to equal suffrage.

The Sixteenth Amendment overrode the Supreme Court's decision in *Pollock* v. *Farmers' Loan & Trust Co.* (1895), that a tax on incomes derived from property was a direct tax, and empowered Congress to impose an income tax without apportionment among the states, as previously required by Article I, Section 9.

The Seventeenth Amendment relieved the state legislatures of the time-consuming duty of electing United States Senators and improved the representative quality of the Senate by making its members popularly elective.

The Eighteenth Amendment prohibited the manufacture, sale, or transportation of intoxicating liquors and gave Congress and state legislatures concurrent power to enforce the Amendment.

The Nineteenth Amendment forbade a state to deny suffrage because of sex, thus enfranchising women on the same terms as men.

The Twentieth Amendment moved back the beginning of congressional terms from March 4 to January 3, and of presidential terms to January 20; required a new Congress to meet January 3, two months after its election, instead of eleven months, as formerly; and provided for succession to the presidency in certain contingencies.

The Twenty-first Amendment repealed the Eighteenth.

The Twenty-second Amendment limits the President to two terms in office, restoring the limitation by custom that had existed from the end of Washington's second term until the election of Franklin D. Roosevelt for third and fourth terms.

The Twenty-third Amendment enables the voters of the District of Columbia to elect as many presidential electors as the District would be entitled to if it were a state, but not more than the least populous state.

The Twenty-fourth Amendment forbids the denial of the suffrage in primary or other elections for federal officers because of failure to pay a poll tax or any other tax. (The poll tax requirement in *state* elections was later declared unconstitutional by the Supreme Court, in *Harper* v. *Virginia State Board of Elections* [1966].)

The Twenty-fifth Amendment provides that the Vice President shall become Acting President whenever the President states that he is unable to perform his duties, or a similar statement is made by a body authorized by Congress to determine questions of presidential disability. If there is disagreement between this body and the President, Congress must decide the issue within twenty-one days and, by a two-thirds vote of both houses, may declare that the President is unable to perform his duties.

The Twenty-sixth Amendment extends the suffrage in both state and national elections to all citizens eighteen years old and over. It was adopted after the Supreme Court, in *Oregon* v. *Mitchell* (1970), declared unconstitutional the provisions of the Voting Rights Act insofar as they related to state elections.

DOCUMENTS

VIRGINIA BILL OF RIGHTS*
Adopted June 12, 1776

A declaration of rights made by the representatives of the good people of Virginia, assembled in full and free convention; which rights do pertain to them and their posterity, as the basis and foundation of government.

SECTION 1.   That all men are by nature equally free and independent, and have certain inherent rights, of which, when they enter into a state of society, they cannot, by any compact, deprive or divest their posterity; namely, the enjoyment of life and liberty, with the means of acquiring and possessing property, and pursuing and obtaining happiness and safety.

SECTION 2.   That all power is vested in, and consequently derived from, the people; that magistrates are their trustees and servants, and at all times amenable to them.

SECTION 3.   That government is, or ought to be, instituted for the common benefit, protection, and security of the people, nation, or community; of all the various modes and forms of government, that is best which is capable of producing the greatest degree of happiness and safety, and is most effectually secured against the danger of maladministration; and that, when any government shall be found inadequate or contrary to these purposes, a majority of the community hath an indubitable, inalienable, and infeasible right to reform, alter, or abolish it, in such manner as shall be judged most conducive to the public weal.

SECTION 4.   That no man, or set of men, are entitled to exclusive or separate emoluments or privileges from the community, but in consideration of public services; which, not being descendible, neither ought the offices of magistrate, legislator, or judge to be hereditary.

* B. P. Poore, ed., *The Federal and States Constitutions, Colonial Charters, and Other Organic Laws of the United States* (2nd ed., Washington, D.C.: Government Printing Office, 1878), II, 1908 ff.

SECTION 5.   That the legislative and executive powers of the State should be separate and distinct from the judiciary; and that the members of the two first may be restrained from oppression, by feeling and participating the burdens of the people, they should, at fixed periods, be reduced to a private station, return into that body from which they were originally taken, and the vacancies be supplied by frequent, certain, and regular elections, in which all, or any part of the former members, to be again eligible, or ineligible, as the laws shall direct.

SECTION 6.   That elections of members to serve as representatives of the people in assembly, ought to be free; and that all men, having sufficient evidence of permanent common interest with, and attachment to, the community, have the right of suffrage, and cannot be taxed or deprived of their property for public uses, without their own consent, or that of their representatives so elected, nor bound by any law to which they have not, in like manner, assented, for the public good.

SECTION 7.   That all power of suspending laws, or the execution of laws, by any authority, without consent of the representatives of the people, is injurious to their rights, and ought not to be exercised.

SECTION 8.   That in all capital or criminal prosecutions a man hath a right to demand the cause and nature of his accusation, to be confronted with the accusers and witnesses, to call for evidence in his favor, and to a speedy trial by an impartial jury of twelve men of his vicinage, without whose unanimous consent he cannot be found guilty; nor can he be compelled to give evidence against himself; that no man be deprived of his liberty, except by the law of the land or the judgment of his peers.

SECTION 9.   That excessive bail ought not to be required, nor excessive fines imposed, nor cruel and unusual punishment inflicted.

SECTION 10.   That general warrants, whereby an officer or messenger may be commanded to search suspected places without evidence of a fact committed, or to seize any person or persons not named, or whose offence is not particularly described and supported by evidence, are grievous and oppressive, and ought not to be granted.

SECTION 11.   That in controversies respecting property, and in suits between man and man, the ancient trial by jury is preferable to any other, and ought to be held sacred.

SECTION 12.   That the freedom of the press is one of the great bulwarks of liberty, and can never be restrained but by despotic governments.

SECTION 13.   That a well-regulated militia, composed of the body of the people, trained to arms, is the proper, natural, and safe defence of a free State; that standing armies, in time of peace, should be avoided, as dangerous to liberty; and that in all cases the military should be under strict subordination to, and governed by, the civil power.

SECTION 14. That the people have a right to uniform government; and, therefore, that no government separate from, or independent of the government of Virginia, ought to be erected or established within the limits thereof.

SECTION 15. That no free government, or the blessings of liberty, can be preserved to any people, but by a firm adherence to justice, moderation, temperance, frugality, and virtue, and by frequent recurrence to fundamental principles.

SECTION 16. That religion, or the duty which we owe to our Creator, and the manner of discharging it, can be directed only by reason and conviction, not by force or violence; and therefore all men are equally entitled to the free exercise of religion, according to the dictates of conscience; and that it is the mutual duty of all to practise Christian forbearance, love, and charity towards each other.

A DECLARATION
by the Representatives of the
United States of America
in General Congress Assembled
July 4, 1776

When, in the course of human events, it becomes necessary for one people to dissolve the political bands which have connected them with another, and to assume, among the powers of the earth, the separate and equal station to which the laws of nature and of nature's God entitle them, a decent respect to the opinions of mankind requires that they should declare the causes which impel them to the separation.

We hold these truths to be self-evident, that all men are created equal; that they are endowed by their Creator with certain inalienable rights; that among these, are life, liberty, and the pursuit of happiness. That, to secure these rights, governments are instituted among men, deriving their just powers from the consent of the governed; that, whenever any form of government becomes destructive of these ends, it is the right of the people to alter or to abolish it, and to institute a new government, laying its foundation on such principles, and organizing its powers in such form, as to them shall seem most likely to effect their safety and happiness. Prudence, indeed, will dictate that governments long established, should not be changed for light and transient causes; and, accordingly, all experience hath shown, that mankind are more disposed to suffer, while evils are sufferable, than to right themselves by abolishing the forms to which they are accustomed. But, when a long train of abuses and usurpations, pursuing invariably the same object, evinces a design to reduce them under absolute despotism, it is their right, it is their duty, to throw off such government and to provide new guards for their future security. Such has been the patient sufferance of these colonies, and such is now the necessity which constrains them to alter their former systems of government. The history of the present King of Great Britain is a history of repeated injuries and usurpations, all having, in direct object, the establishment of an absolute tyranny over these States. To prove this, let facts be submitted to a candid world:—

He has refused his assent to laws the most wholesome and necessary for the public good.

He has forbidden his governors to pass laws of immediate and pressing importance, unless suspended in their operation till his assent should be obtained; and, when so suspended, he has utterly neglected to attend to them.

He has refused to pass other laws for the accommodation of large districts of people, unless those people would relinquish the right of representation in the legislature: a right inestimable to them, and formidable to tyrants only.

He has called together legislative bodies at places unusual, uncomfortable, and distant from the depository of their public records, for the sole purpose of fatiguing them into compliance with his measures.

He has dissolved representative houses repeatedly for opposing, with manly firmness, his invasions on the rights of the people.

He has refused, for a long time after such dissolutions, to cause others to be elected; whereby the legislative powers, incapable of annihilation, have returned to the people at large for their exercise; the state remaining, in the meantime, exposed to all the danger of invasion from without, and convulsions within.

He has endeavored to prevent the population of these States; for that purpose, obstructing the laws for naturalization of foreigners, refusing to pass others to encourage their migration hither, and raising the conditions of new appropriations of lands.

He has obstructed the administration of justice, by refusing his assent to laws for establishing judiciary powers.

He has made judges dependent on his will alone, for the tenure of their offices, and the amount and payment of their salaries.

He has erected a multitude of new offices, and sent hither swarms of officers, to harass our people, and eat out their substance.

He has kept among us, in time of peace, standing armies, without the consent of our legislatures.

He has affected to render the military independent of, and superior to, the civil power.

He has combined, with others, to subject us to a jurisdiction foreign to our Constitution, and unacknowledged by our laws; giving his assent to their acts of pretended legislation:

For quartering large bodies of armed troops among us:

For protecting them by a mock trial, from punishment, for any murders which they should commit on the inhabitants of these States:

For cutting off our trade with all parts of the world:

For imposing taxes on us without our consent:

For depriving us, in many cases, of the benefit of trial by jury:

For transporting us beyond seas to be tried for pretended offenses:

For abolishing the free system of English laws in a neighboring province, establishing therein an arbitrary government, and enlarging its boundaries, so as to render it at once an example and fit instrument for introducing the same absolute rule into these colonies:

For taking away our charters, abolishing our most valuable laws, and altering, fundamentally, the powers of our governments:

For suspending our own legislatures, and declaring themselves invested with power to legislate for us in all cases whatsoever.

He has abdicated government here, by declaring us out of his protection, and waging war against us.

He has plundered our seas, ravaged our coasts, burnt our towns, and destroyed the lives of our people.

He is, at this time, transporting large armies of foreign mercenaries to complete the works of death, desolation, and tyranny, already begun, with circumstances of cruelty and perfidy scarcely paralleled in the most barbarous ages, and totally unworthy the head of a civilized nation.

He has constrained our fellow citizens, taken captive on the high seas, to bear arms against their country, to become the executioners of their friends, and brethren, or to fall themselves by their hands.

He has excited domestic insurrections amongst us, and has endeavored to bring on the inhabitants of our frontiers, the merciless Indian savages, whose known rule of warfare is an undistinguished destruction of all ages, sexes, and conditions.

In every stage of these oppressions, we have petitioned for redress, in the most humble terms; our repeated petitions have been answered only by repeated injury. A prince, whose character is thus marked by every act which may define a tyrant, is unfit to be the ruler of a free people.

Nor have we been wanting in attention to our British brethren. We have warned them, from time to time, of attempts made by their legislature to extend an unwarrantable jurisdiction over us. We have reminded them of the circumstances of our emigration and settlement here. We have appealed to their native justice and magnanimity, and we have conjured them, by the ties of our common kindred, to disavow these usurpations, which would inevitably interrupt our connections and correspondence. They, too, have been deaf to the voice of justice and consanguinity. We must, therefore, acquiesce in the necessity which denounces our separation, and hold them, as we hold the rest of mankind, enemies in war, in peace, friends.

We, therefore, the representatives of the United States of America, in general Congress assembled, appealing to the Supreme Judge of the world for the rectitude of our intentions, do, in the name, and by the authority of the good people of these colonies, solemnly publish and declare, that these united colonies are, and of right ought to be, free and independent states: that they are absolved from all allegiance to the British Crown, and that all political connection between them and the state of Great Britain is, and ought to be, totally dissolved; and that, as free and independent states, they have full power to levy war, conclude peace, contract alliances, establish commerce, and to do all other acts and things which independent states may of right do. And, for the support of this declaration, with a firm reliance on the protection of Divine Providence, we mutually pledge to each other our lives, our fortunes, and our sacred honor.

ARTICLES OF CONFEDERATION

Proposed by Congress November 15, 1777
Ratified and effective March 1, 1781

To all to whom these Presents shall come, we the undersigned Delegates of the States affixed to our Names send greeting.

Whereas the Delegates of the United States of America, in Congress assembled, did, on the fifteenth day of November in the Year of our Lord One Thousand Seven Hundred and Seventy seven, and in the Second Year of the Independence of America, agree to certain articles of Confederation and perpetual Union between the States of Newhampshire, Massachusetts-bay, Rhodeisland and Providence Plantations, Connecticut, New York, New Jersey, Pennsylvania, Delaware, Maryland, Virginia, North-Carolina, South-Carolina, and Georgia in the words following, viz. "Articles of Confederation and perpetual Union between the states of Newhampshire, Massachusetts-bay, Rhodeisland and Providence Plantations, Connecticut, New-York, New-Jersey, Pennsylvania, Delaware, Maryland, Virginia, North-Carolina, South-Carolina and Georgia.

ARTICLE I. The Stile of this Confederacy shall be "The United States of America."

ARTICLE II. Each state retains its sovereignty, freedom, and independence, and every Power, Jurisdiction and right, which is not by this confederation expressly delegated to the United States, in Congress assembled.

ARTICLE III. The said states hereby severally enter into a firm league of friendship with each other, for their common defence, the security of their Liberties, and their mutual and general welfare, binding themselves to assist each other, against all force offered to, or attacks made upon them, or any of them, on account of religion, sovereignty, trade, or any other pretence whatever.

ARTICLE IV.   The better to secure and perpetuate mutual friendship and intercourse among the people of the different states in this union, the free inhabitants of each of these states, paupers, vagabonds and fugitives from justice excepted, shall be entitled to all privileges and immunities of free citizens in the several states; and the people of each state shall have free ingress and regress to and from any other state, and shall enjoy therein all the privileges of trade and commerce, subject to the same duties, impositions and restrictions as the inhabitants thereof respectively, provided that such restrictions shall not extend so far as to prevent the removal of property imported into any state, to any other state of which the Owner is an inhabitant; provided also that no imposition, duties or restrictions shall be laid by any state, on the property of the united states, or either of them.

If any Person guilty of, or charged with treason, felony, or other high misdeameanor in any state, shall flee from Justice, and be found in any of the united states, he shall, upon demand of the Governor or executive power, of the state from which he fled, be delivered up and removed to the state having jurisdiction of his offence.

Full faith and credit shall be given in each of these states to the records, acts and judicial proceedings of the courts and magistrates of every other state.

ARTICLE V.   For the more convenient management of the general interests of the united states, delegates shall be annually appointed in such manner as the legislature of each state shall direct, to meet in Congress on the first Monday in November, in every year, with a power reserved to each state, to recall its delegates, or any of them, at any time within the year, and to send others in their stead, for the remainder of the Year.

No state shall be represented in Congress by less than two, nor by more than seven Members; and no person shall be capable of being a delegate for more than three years in any term of six years; nor shall any person, being a delegate, be capable of holding any office under the united states, for which he, or another of his benefit receives any salary, fees or emolument of any kind.

Each state shall maintain its own delegates in a meeting of the states, and while they act as members of the committee of the states.

In determining questions in the united states in Congress assembled, each state shall have one vote.

Freedom of speech and debate in Congress shall not be impeached or questioned in any Court, or place out of Congress, and the members of congress shall be protected in their persons from arrests and imprisonments, during the time of their going to and from, and attendance on Congress, except for treason, felony, or breach of the peace.

ARTICLE VI. No state without the Consent of the united states in congress assembled, shall send any embassy to, or receive any embassy from, or enter into any conference, agreement, alliance or treaty with any King, prince or state; nor shall any person holding any office of profit or trust under the united states, or any of them, accept of any present, emolument, office or title of any kind whatever from any king, prince or foreign state; nor shall the united states in congress assembled, or any of them, grant any title of nobility.

No two or more states shall enter into any treaty, confederation or alliance whatever between them, without the consent of the united states in congress assembled, specifying accurately the purposes for which the same is to be entered into, and how long it shall continue.

No state shall lay any imposts or duties, which may interfere with any stipulations in treaties, entered into by the United States in Congress assembled, with any king, prince or state, in pursuance of any treaties already proposed by congress, to the courts of France and Spain.

No vessels of war shall be kept up in time of peace by any state, except such number only, as shall be deemed necessary by the united states in congress assembled, for the defence of such state, or its trade; nor shall any body of forces be kept up by any state, in time of peace, except such number only, as in the judgment of the united states, in congress assembled, shall be deemed requisite to garrison the forts necessary for the defence of such state; but every state shall always keep up a well regulated and disciplined militia, sufficiently armed and accoutred, and shall provide and constantly have ready for use, in public stores, a due number of field pieces and tents, and a proper quantity of arms, ammunition and camp equipage.

No state shall engage in any war without the consent of the united states in congress assembled, unless such state be actually invaded by enemies, or shall have received certain advice of a resolution being formed by some nation of Indians to invade such state, and the danger is so imminent as not to admit of a delay till the united states in congress assembled can be consulted: nor shall any state grant commissions to any ships or vessels of war, nor letters of marque or reprisal, except it be after a declaration of war by the united states in congress assembled, and then only against the kingdom or state and the subjects thereof, against which war has been so declared, and under such regulations as shall be established by the united states in congress assembled, unless such state be infested by pirates, in which case vessels of war may be fitted out for that occasion, and kept so long as the danger shall continue, or until the united states in congress assembled, shall determine otherwise.

ARTICLE VII. When land-forces are raised by any state for the common defence, all officers of or under the rank of colonel, shall be appointed by the legislature of each state respectively, by whom such forces shall be raised, or in such manner as such state shall direct, and all vacancies shall be filled up by the State which first made the appointment.

ARTICLE VIII. All charges of war, and all other expences that shall be incurred for the common defence or general welfare, and allowed by the united states in congress assembled, shall be defrayed out of a common treasury, which shall be supplied by the several states in proportion to the value of all land within each state, granted to or surveyed for any Person, as such land and the buildings and improvements thereon shall be estimated according to such mode as the united states in congress assembled, shall from time to time direct and appoint.

The taxes for paying that proportion shall be laid and levied by the authority and direction of the legislatures of the several states within the time agreed upon by the United States in Congress assembled.

ARTICLE IX. The united states in congress assembled, shall have the sole and exclusive right and power of determining on peace and war, except in the cases mentioned in the sixth article—of sending and receiving ambassadors—entering into treaties and alliances, provided that no treaty of commerce shall be made whereby the legislative power of the respective states shall be restrained from imposing such imposts and duties on foreigners as their own people are subjected to, or from prohibiting the exploration or importation of any species of goods or commodities, whatsoever—of establishing rules for deciding in all cases, what captures on land or water shall be legal, and in what manner prizes taken by land or naval forces in the service of the united states shall be divided or appropriated—of granting letters of marque and reprisal in times of peace—appointing courts for the trial of piracies and felonies committed on the high seas and establishing courts for receiving and determining finally appeals in all cases of captures, provided that no member of congress shall be appointed a judge of any of the said courts.

The united states in congress assembled shall also be the last resort on appeal in all disputes and differences now subsisting or that hereafter may arise between two or more states concerning boundary, jurisdiction or any other cause whatever; which authority shall always be exercised in the manner following. Whenever the legislative or executive authority or lawful agent of any state in controversy with another shall present a petition to congress stating the matter in question and praying for a hearing, notice thereof shall be given by order of congress to the legislative or executive authority of the other state in controversy, and a day assigned for the appearance of the parties by their lawful agents, who shall then be directed to appoint by joint consent, commissioners or judges to constitute a court for hearing and determining the matter in question: but if they cannot agree, congress shall name three persons out of each of the united states, and from the list of such persons each party shall alternately strike out one, the petitioners beginning, until the number shall be reduced to thirteen; and from that number not less than seven, nor more than nine names as congress shall direct, shall in the presence of congress be drawn out by lot, and the persons whose names shall be so drawn or any five of them, shall be commissioners or judges, to hear and finally determine the controversy, so always as a major part of the judges who shall hear the cause shall agree in the determination: and if either party shall neglect to attend at the day appointed, without showing reasons, which congress shall judge sufficient, or being present shall refuse to strike, the congress shall proceed to nominate three persons out of each state, and the secretary of congress shall strike in behalf of such party absent or refusing; and the judgment and sentence of the court to be appointed, in the manner before prescribed, shall be final and conclusive; and if any of the parties shall refuse to submit to the authority of such court, or to appear or defend their claim or cause, the court shall nevertheless proceed to pronounce sentence, or judgment, which shall in like manner be final and decisive, the judgment or sentence and other proceedings being in either case transmitted to congress, and lodged among the acts of congress for the security of the parties concerned: provided that every commissioner, before he sits in judgment, shall take an oath to be administered by one of the judges of the supreme or superior court of the state where the cause shall be tried, "well and truly to hear and determine the matter in question, according to the best of his judgment, without favour, affection or hope of reward:" provided also, that no state shall be deprived of territory for the benefit of the united states.

All controversies concerning the private right of soil claimed under different grants of two or more states, whose jurisdictions as they may respect such lands, and the states which passed such grants are adjusted, the said grants or either of them being at the same time claimed to have originated antecedent to such settlement of jurisdiction, shall on the petition of either party to the congress of the united states, be finally determined as near as may be in the same manner as is before prescribed for deciding disputes respecting territorial jurisdiction between different states.

The united states in congress assembled shall also have the sole and exclusive right and power of regulating the alloy and value of coin struck by their own authority, or by that of the respective states— fixing the standard of weights and measures throughout the united states—regulating the trade and managing all affairs with the Indians, not members of any of the states, provided that the legislative right of any state within its own limits be not infringed or violated—establishing and regulating post-offices from one state to another, throughout all the united states, and exacting such postage on the papers passing thro' the same as may be requisite to defray the expences of the said office— appointing all officers of the land forces, in the service of the united states, excepting regimental officers—appointing all the officers of the naval forces, and commissioning all officers whatever in the service of the united states—making rules for the government and regulation of the said land and naval forces, and directing their operations.

The united states in congress assembled shall have authority to appoint a committee, to sit in the recess of congress, to be denominated "A Committee of the States," and to consist of one delegate from each state; and to appoint such other committees and civil officers as may be necessary for managing the general affairs of the united states under their direction—to appoint one of their number to preside, provided that no person be allowed to serve in the office of president more than one year in any term of three years; to ascertain the necessary sums of money to be raised for the service of the united states, and to appropriate and apply the same for defraying the public expences—to borrow money, or emit bills on the credit of the united states, transmitting every half year to the respective states an account of the sums of money so borrowed or emitted,—to build and equip a navy—to agree upon the number of land forces, and to make requisitions from each state for its quota, in proportion to the number of white inhabitants in such state; which requisition shall be binding, and thereupon the legislature of each state shall appoint the regimental officers, raise the men and cloath, arm and equip them in a soldier like manner, at the expence of the united states; and the officers and men so cloathed, armed and equipped shall march to the place appointed, and within the time agreed on by the united states in congress assembled: But if the united states in congress assembled shall, on consideration of circumstances judge proper that any state should not raise men, or should raise a smaller number than its quota, and that any other state should raise a greater number of men than the quota thereof, such extra number shall be raised, officered, cloathed, armed and equipped in the same manner as the quota of such state, unless the legislature of such state shall judge that such extra number cannot be safely spared out of the same, in which case they shall raise officer, cloath, arm and equip as many of such extra number as they judge can be safely spared. And the officers and men so cloathed, armed and equipped, shall march to the place appointed, and within the time agreed on by the united states in congress assembled.

The united states in congress assembled shall never engage in a war, nor grant letters of marque and reprisal in time of peace, nor enter into any treaties or alliances, nor coin money, nor regulate the value thereof, nor ascertain the sums and expences necessary for the defence and welfare of the united states, or any of them, nor emit bills, nor borrow money on the credit of the united states, nor appropriate money, nor agree upon the number of vessels of war, to be built or purchased, or the number of land or sea forces to be raised, nor appoint a commander in chief of the army or navy, unless nine states assent to the same: nor shall a question on any other point, except for adjourning from day to day be determined, unless by the votes of a majority of the united states in congress assembled.

The congress of the united states shall have power to adjourn to any time within the year, and to any place within the united states, so that no period of adjournment be for a longer duration than the space of six Months, and shall publish the Journal of their proceedings monthly, except such parts thereof relating to treaties, alliances or military operations, as in their judgment require secrecy; and the yeas and nays of the delegates of each state on any question shall be entered on the Journal, when it is desired by any delegate; and the delegates of a state, or any of them, at his or their request shall be furnished with a transcript of the said Journal, except such parts as are above excepted, to lay before the legislatures of the several states.

ARTICLE X.   The committee of the states, or any nine of them, shall be authorized to execute, in the recess of congress, such of the powers of congress as the united states in congress assembled, by the consent of nine states, shall from time to time think expedient to vest them with; provided that no power be delegated to the said committee, for the exercise of which, by the articles of confederation, the voice of nine states in the congress of the united states assembled is requisite.

ARTICLE XI.   Canada acceding to this confederation, and joining in the measures of the united states, shall be admitted into, and entitled to all the advantages of this union: but no other colony shall be admitted into the same, unless such admission be agreed to by nine states.

ARTICLE XII.   All bills of credit emitted, monies borrowed and debts contracted by, or under the authority of Congress, before the assembling of the united states, in pursuance of the present confederation, shall be deemed and considered as a charge against the united states, for payment and satisfaction whereof the said united states, and the public faith are hereby solemnly pledged.

ARTICLE XIII.   Every state shall abide by the determinations of the united states in congress assembled, on all questions which by this confederation are submitted to them. And the Articles of this confederation shall be inviolably observed by every state, and the union shall be perpetual; nor shall any alteration at any time hereafter be made in any of them; unless such alteration be agreed to in a congress of the united states, and be afterwards confirmed by the legislatures of every state.

And Whereas it has pleased the Great Governor of the World to incline the hearts of the legislatures we respectively represent in congress, to approve of, and to authorize us to ratify the said articles of confederation and perpetual union. Know Ye that we the undersigned delegates, by virtue of the power and authority to us given for that purpose, do by these presents, in the name and in behalf of our respective constituents, fully and entirely ratify and confirm each and every of the said articles of confederation and perpetual union, and all and singular the matters and things therein contained: And we do further solemnly plight and engage the faith of our respective constituents, that they shall abide by the determinations of the united states in congress assembled, on all questions, which by the said confederation are submitted to them. And that the articles thereof shall be inviolably observed by the states we respectively represent, and that the union shall be perpetual. In Witness whereof we have hereunto set our hands in Congress. Done at Philadelphia in the state of Pennsylvania the ninth day of July, in the year of our Lord one Thousand seven Hundred and Seventy-eight, and in the third year of the independence of America. [Names omitted]

CONSTITUTION
OF THE UNITED STATES

Proposed by Convention September 17, 1787
Effective March 4, 1789

WE the people of the United States, in order to form a more perfect union, establish justice, insure domestic tranquillity, provide for the common defense, promote the general welfare, and secure the blessings of liberty to ourselves and our posterity, do ordain and establish this Constitution for the United States of America.

ARTICLE I

SECTION 1.   All legislative powers herein granted shall be vested in a Congress of the United States, which shall consist of a Senate and House of Representatives.

SECTION 2.   1.   The House of Representatives shall be composed of members chosen every second year by the people of the several States, and the electors in each State shall have the qualifications requisite for electors of the most numerous branch of the State legislature.

2.   No person shall be a representative who shall not have attained to the age of twenty-five years, and been seven years a citizen of the United States, and who shall not, when elected, be an inhabitant of that State in which he shall be chosen.

3.   Representatives [and direct taxes]* shall be apportioned among the several States which may be included within this Union, according to their respective numbers, [which shall be determined by adding to the whole number of free persons, including those bound to service for a term of years, and excluding Indians not taxed, three fifths of all other persons.]† The actual enumeration shall be made within three

* See the 16th Amendment.
† See the 14th Amendment.

37

years after the first meeting of the Congress of the United States, and within every subsequent term of ten years, in such manner as they shall by law direct. The number of representatives shall not exceed one for every thirty thousand, but each State shall have at least one representative; and until such enumeration shall be made, the State of New Hampshire shall be entitled to choose three, Massachusetts eight, Rhode Island and Providence Plantations one, Connecticut five, New York six, New Jersey four, Pennsylvania eight, Delaware one, Maryland six, Virginia ten, North Carolina five, South Carolina five, and Georgia three.

4. When vacancies happen in the representation from any State, the executive authority thereof shall issue writs of election to fill such vacancies.

5. The House of Representatives shall choose their speaker and other officers; and shall have the sole power of impeachment.

SECTION 3. 1. The Senate of the United States shall be composed of two senators from each State, [chosen by the legislature thereof,]* for six years; and each senator shall have one vote.

2. Immediately after they shall be assembled in consequence of the first election, they shall be divided as equally as may be into three classes. The seats of the senators of the first class shall be vacated at the expiration of the second year, of the second class at the expiration of the fourth year, and of the third class at the expiration of the sixth year, so that one third may be chosen every second year; and if vacancies happen by resignation, or otherwise, during the recess of the legislature of any State, the executive thereof may make temporary appointments until the next meeting of the legislature, which shall then fill such vacancies.*

3. No person shall be a senator who shall not have attained to the age of thirty years, and been nine years a citizen of the United States, and who shall not, when elected, be an inhabitant of that State for which he shall be chosen.

4. The Vice President of the United States shall be President of the Senate, but shall have no vote, unless they be equally divided.

5. The Senate shall choose their other officers, and also a president *pro tempore,* in the absence of the Vice President, or when he shall exercise the office of the President of the United States.

6. The Senate shall have the sole power to try all impeachments. When sitting for that purpose, they shall be on oath or affirmation.

* See the 17th Amendment.

When the President of the United States is tried, the chief justice shall preside: and no person shall be convicted without the concurrence of two thirds of the members present.

7.   Judgment in cases of impeachment shall not extend further than to removal from office, and disqualifications to hold and enjoy any office of honor, trust or profit under the United States: but the party convicted shall nevertheless be liable and subject to indictment, trial, judgment and punishment, according to law.

SECTION 4.   1.   The times, places, and manner of holding elections for senators and representatives, shall be prescribed in each State by the legislature thereof; but the Congress may at any time by law make or alter such regulations, except as to the places of choosing senators.

2.   The Congress shall assemble at least once in every year, and such meeting shall be on the first Monday in December,* unless they shall by law appoint a different day.

SECTION 5.   1.   Each House shall be the judge of the elections, returns and qualifications of its own members, and a majority of each shall constitute a quorum to do business; but a smaller number may adjourn from day to day, and may be authorized to compel the attendance of absent members, in such manner, and under such penalties as each House may provide.

2.   Each House may determine the rules of its proceedings, punish its members for disorderly behavior, and, with the concurrence of two thirds, expel a member.

3.   Each House shall keep a journal of its proceedings, and from time to time publish the same, excepting such parts as may in their judgment require secrecy; and the yeas and nays of the members of either House on any question shall, at the desire of one fifth of those present, be entered on the journal.

4.   Neither House, during the session of Congress, shall, without the consent of the other, adjourn for more than three days, nor to any other place than that in which the two Houses shall be sitting.

SECTION 6.   1.   The senators and representatives shall receive a compensation for their services, to be ascertained by law, and paid out of the Treasury of the United States. They shall in all cases, except treason, felony, and breach of the peace, be privileged from arrest during their attendance at the session of their respective Houses, and in going to and returning from the same; and for any speech or debate in either House, they shall not be questioned in any other place.

* Modified by the 20th Amendment.

2. No senator or representative shall, during the time for which he was elected, be appointed to any civil office under the authority of the United States, which shall have been created, or the emoluments whereof shall have been increased during such time; and no person holding any office under the United States shall be a member of either House during his continuance in office.

SECTION 7. 1. All bills for raising revenue shall originate in the House of Representatives; but the Senate may propose or concur with amendments as on other bills.

2. Every bill which shall have passed the House of Representatives and the Senate, shall, before it becomes a law, be presented to the President of the United States; if he approves he shall sign it, but if not he shall return it, with his objections to that House in which it shall have originated, who shall enter the objections at large on their journal, and proceed to reconsider it. If after such reconsideration two thirds of that House shall agree to pass the bill, it shall be sent, together with the objections, to the other House, by which it shall likewise be reconsidered, and if approved by two thirds of that House, it shall become a law. But in all such cases the votes of both Houses shall be determined by yeas and nays, and the names of the persons voting for and against the bill shall be entered on the journal of each House respectively. If any bill shall not be returned by the President within ten days (Sundays excepted) after it shall have been presented to him, the same shall be a law, in like manner as if he had signed it, unless the Congress by their adjournment prevent its return, in which case it shall not be a law.

3. Every order, resolution, or vote to which the concurrence of the Senate and the House of Representatives may be necessary (except on a question of adjournment) shall be presented to the President of the United States; and before the same shall take effect, shall be approved by him, or being disapproved by him, shall be repassed by two thirds of the Senate and House of Representatives, according to the rules and limitations prescribed in the case of a bill.

SECTION 8. The Congress shall have the power

1. To lay and collect taxes, duties, imposts, and excises, to pay the debts and provide for the common defense and general welfare of the United States; but all duties, imposts, and excises shall be uniform throughout the United States;

2. To borrow money on the credit of the United States;

3. To regulate commerce with foreign nations, and among the several States, and with the Indian tribes;

4. To establish a uniform rule of naturalization, and uniform laws on the subject of bankruptcies throughout the United States;

5. To coin money, regulate the value thereof, and of foreign coin, and fix the standard of weights and measures;

6. To provide for the punishment of counterfeiting the securities and current coin of the United States;

7. To establish post offices and post roads;

8. To promote the progress of science and useful arts, by securing for limited times to authors and inventors the exclusive right to their respective writings and discoveries;

9. To constitute tribunals inferior to the Supreme Court;

10. To define and punish piracies and felonies committed on the high seas, and offenses against the law of nations;

11. To declare war, grant letters of marque and reprisal, and make rules concerning captures on land and water;

12. To raise and support armies, but no appropriation of money to that use shall be for a longer term than two years;

13. To provide and maintain a navy;

14. To make rules for the government and regulation of the land and naval forces;

15. To provide for calling forth the militia to execute the laws of the Union, suppress insurrections and repel invasions;

16. To provide for organizing, arming, and disciplining the militia, and for governing such part of them as may be employed in the service of the United States, reserving to the States respectively, the appointment of the officers, and the authority of training the militia according to the discipline prescribed by Congress;

17. To exercise exclusive legislation in all cases whatsoever, over such district (not exceeding ten miles square) as may, by cession of particular States, and the acceptance of Congress, become the seat of the government of the United States, and to exercise like authority over all places purchased by the consent of the legislature of the State in which the same shall be, for the erection of forts, magazines, arsenals, dockyards, and other needful buildings; and

18. To make all laws which shall be necessary and proper for carrying into execution the foregoing powers, and all other powers vested by this Constitution in the government of the United States, or in any department or officer thereof.

SECTION 9.   1.   The migration or importation of such persons as any of the States now existing shall think proper to admit, shall not be prohibited by the Congress prior to the year one thousand eight hundred and eight, but a tax or duty may be imposed on such importation, not exceeding ten dollars for each person.

2.   The privilege of the writ of *habeas corpus* shall not be suspended, unless when in cases of rebellion or invasion the public safety may require it.

3.   No bill of attainder or *ex post facto* law shall be passed.

4.   No capitation, or other direct, tax shall be laid unless in proportion to the census or enumeration hereinbefore directed to be taken.*

5.   No tax or duty shall be laid on articles exported from any State.

6.   No preference shall be given by any regulation of commerce or revenue to the ports of one State over those of another: nor shall vessels bound to, or from, one State be obliged to enter, clear, or pay duties in another.

7.   No money shall be drawn from the treasury, but in consequence of appropriations made by law; and a regular statement and account of the receipts and expenditures of all public money shall be published from time to time.

8.   No title of nobility shall be granted by the United States: and no person holding any office of profit or trust under them, shall, without the consent of the Congress, accept of any present, emolument, office, or title, of any kind whatever, from any king, prince, or foreign State.

SECTION 10.   1.   No State shall enter into any treaty, alliance, or confederation; grant letters of marque and reprisal; coin money; emit bills of credit; make anything but gold and silver coin a tender in payment of debts; pass any bill of attainder, *ex post facto* law, or law impairing the obligation of contracts, or grant any title of nobility.

2.   No State shall, without the consent of the Congress, lay any imposts or duties on imports or exports, except what may be absolutely necessary for executing its inspection laws; and the net produce of all duties and imposts laid by any State on imports or exports, shall be for the use of the treasury of the United States; and all such laws shall be subject to the revision and control of the Congress.

3.   No State shall, without the consent of the Congress, lay any duty of tonnage, keep troops, or ships of war in time of peace, enter into any agreement or compact with another State, or with a foreign

* See the 16th Amendment.

power, or engage in war, unless actually invaded, or in such imminent danger as will not admit of delay.

ARTICLE II

SECTION 1.   1.   The executive power shall be vested in a President of the United States of America. He shall hold his office during the term of four years, and, together with the Vice President, chosen for the same term, be elected as follows:

2.   Each State* shall appoint, in such manner as the legislature thereof may direct, a number of electors, equal to the whole number of senators and representatives to which the State may be entitled in the Congress: but no senator or representative, or person holding an office of trust or profit under the United States, shall be appointed an elector.

The electors shall meet in their respective States, and vote by ballot for two persons, of whom one at least shall not be an inhabitant of the same State with themselves. And they shall make a list of all the persons voted for, and of the number of votes for each; which list they shall sign and certify, and transmit sealed to the seat of the government of the United States, directed to the president of the Senate. The president of the Senate shall, in the presence of the Senate and House of Representatives, open all the certificates, and the votes shall then be counted. The person having the greatest number of votes shall be the President, if such number be a majority of the whole number of electors appointed; and if there be more than one who have such majority, and have an equal number of votes, then the House of Representatives shall immediately choose by ballot one of them for President; and if no person have a majority, then from the five highest on the list the said House shall in like manner choose the President. But in choosing the President, the votes shall be taken by States, the representation from each State having one vote; a quorum for this purpose shall consist of a member or members from two thirds of the States, and a majority of all the States shall be necessary to a choice. In every case, after the choice of the President, the person having the greatest number of votes of the electors shall be the Vice President. But if there should remain two or more who have equal votes, the Senate shall choose from them by ballot the Vice President.†

* See 23rd Amendment.
† This paragraph was superseded by the 12th Amendment.

3. The Congress may determine the time of choosing the electors, and the day on which they shall give their votes; which day shall be the same throughout the United States.

4. No person except a natural born citizen, or a citizen of the United States, at the time of the adoption of this Constitution, shall be eligible to the office of President; neither shall any person be eligible to that office who shall not have attained to the age of thirty-five years, and been fourteen years a resident within the United States.

5. In case of the removal of the President from office, or of his death, resignation, or inability to discharge the powers and duties of the said office, the same shall devolve on the Vice President, and the Congress may by law provide for the case of removal, death, resignation, or inability, both of the President and Vice President, declaring what officer shall then act as President, and such officer shall act accordingly, until the disability be removed, or a President shall be elected.*

6. The President shall, at stated times, receive for his services a compensation, which shall neither be increased nor diminished during the period for which he shall have been elected, and he shall not receive within that period any other emolument from the United States, or any of them.

7. Before he enter on the execution of his office, he shall take the following oath or affirmation:—"I do solemnly swear (or affirm) that I will faithfully execute the office of President of the United States, and will to the best of my ability, preserve, protect and defend the Constitution of the United States."

SECTION 2. 1. The President shall be commander in chief of the army and navy of the United States, and of the militia of the several States, when called into the actual service of the United States; he may require the opinion, in writing, of the principal officer in each of the executive departments, upon any subject relating to the duties of their respective offices, and he shall have power to grant reprieves and pardons for offenses against the United States, except in cases of impeachment.

2. He shall have power, by and with the advice and consent of the Senate, to make treaties, provided two thirds of the senators present concur; and he shall nominate, and by and with the advice and consent of the Senate, shall appoint ambassadors, other public ministers and consuls, judges of the Supreme Court, and all other officers of the United States, whose appointments are not herein otherwise provided

* See the 25th Amendment.

for, and which shall be established by law: but the Congress may by law vest the appointment of such inferior officers, as they think proper, in the President alone, in the courts of law, or in the heads of departments.

3. The President shall have power to fill up all vacancies that may happen during the recess of the Senate, by granting commissions which shall expire at the end of their next session.

SECTION 3. He shall from time to time give to the Congress information of the state of the Union, and recommend to their consideration such measures as he shall judge necessary and expedient; he may, on extraordinary occasions, convene both Houses, or either of them, and in case of disagreement between them with respect to the time of adjournment, he may adjourn them to such time as he shall think proper; he shall receive ambassadors and other public ministers; he shall take care that the laws be faithfully executed, and shall commission all the officers of the United States.

SECTION 4. The President, Vice President, and all civil officers of the United States, shall be removed from office on impeachment for and conviction of, treason, bribery, or other high crimes and misdemeanors.

ARTICLE III

SECTION 1. The judicial power of the United States shall be vested in one Supreme Court, and in such inferior courts as the Congress may from time to time ordain and establish. The judges, both of the Supreme and inferior courts, shall hold their offices during good behavior, and shall, at stated times, receive for their services, a compensation, which shall not be diminished during their continuance in office.

SECTION 2. 1. The judicial power shall extend to all cases, in law and equity, arising under this Constitution, the laws of the United States, and treaties made, or which shall be made, under their authority; —to all cases affecting ambassadors, other public ministers and consuls; —to all cases of admiralty and maritime jurisdiction;—to controversies to which the United States shall be a party;—to controversies between two or more States;—between a State and citizens of another State;*— between citizens of different States;—between citizens of the same State claiming lands under grants of different States, and between a State, or the citizens thereof, and foreign States, citizens or subjects.

* See the 11th Amendment.

2.   In all cases affecting ambassadors, other public ministers and consuls, and those in which a State shall be party, the Supreme Court shall have original jurisdiction. In all the other cases before mentioned, the Supreme Court shall have appellate jurisdiction, both as to law and to fact, with such exceptions, and under such regulations as the Congress shall make.

3.   The trial of all crimes, except in cases of impeachment, shall be by jury; and such trial shall be held in the State where the said crimes shall have been committed; but when not committed within any State, the trial shall be at such place or places as the Congress may by law have directed.

SECTION 3.   1.   Treason against the United States shall consist only in levying war against them, or in adhering to their enemies, giving them aid and comfort. No person shall be convicted of treason unless on the testimony of two witnesses to the same overt act, or on confession in open court.

2.   The Congress shall have power to declare the punishment of treason, but no attainder of treason shall work corruption of blood, or forfeiture except during the life of the person attained.

ARTICLE IV

SECTION 1.   Full faith and credit shall be given in each State to the public acts, records, and judicial proceedings of every other State. And the Congress may by general laws prescribe the manner in which such acts, records and proceedings shall be proved, and the effect thereof.

SECTION 2.   1.   The citizens of each State shall be entitled to all privileges and immunities of citizens in the several States.*

2.   A person charged in any State with treason, felony, or other crime, who shall flee from justice, and be found in another State, shall on demand of the executive authority of the State from which he fled, be delivered up to be removed to the State having jurisdiction of the crime.

3.   No person held to service or labor in one State under the laws thereof, escaping into another, shall, in consequence of any law or regulation therein, be discharged from such service or labor, but shall

* See the 14th Amendment, Sec. 1.

be delivered up on claim of the party to whom such service or labor may be due.*

SECTION 3.   1.   New States may be admitted by the Congress into this Union; but no new State shall be formed or erected within the jurisdiction of any other State; nor any State be formed by the junction of two or more States, or parts of States, without the consent of the legislatures of the States concerned as well as of the Congress.

2.   The Congress shall have power to dispose of and make all needful rules and regulations respecting the territory or other property belonging to the United States; and nothing in this Constitution shall be so construed as to prejudice any claims of the United States, or of any particular State.

SECTION 4.   The United States shall guarantee to every State in this Union a republican form of government, and shall protect each of them against invasion; and on application of the legislature, or of the executive (when the legislature cannot be convened) against domestic violence.

ARTICLE V

The Congress, whenever two thirds of both Houses shall deem it necessary, shall propose amendments to this Constitution, or, on the application of the legislatures of two thirds of the several States, shall call a convention for proposing amendments, which in either case, shall be valid to all intents and purposes, as part of this Constitution when ratified by the legislatures of three fourths of the several States, or by conventions in three fourths thereof, as the one or the other mode of ratification may be proposed by the Congress; Provided that no amendment which may be made prior to the year one thousand eight hundred and eight shall in any manner affect the first and fourth clauses in the ninth section of the first article; and that no State, without its consent, shall be deprived of its equal suffrage in the Senate.

ARTICLE VI

1.   All debts contracted and engagements entered into, before the adoption of this Constitution, shall be as valid against the United States under this Constitution, as under the Confederation.

2.   This Constitution, and the laws of the United States which shall

* See the 13th Amendment.

be made in pursuance thereof; and all treaties made, or which shall be made, under the authority of the United States, shall be the supreme law of the land; and the Judges in every State shall be bound thereby, anything in the Constitution or laws of any State to the contrary notwithstanding.

3.   The senators and representatives before mentioned, and the members of the several State legislatures, and all executive and judicial officers, both of the United States and of the several States, shall be bound by oath or affirmation to support this Constitution; but no religious test shall ever be required as a qualification to any office or public trust under the United States.

ARTICLE VII

The ratification of the conventions of nine States shall be sufficient for the establishment of this Constitution between the States so ratifying the same.

Done in Convention by the unanimous consent of the States present the seventeenth day of September in the year of our Lord one thousand seven hundred and eighty-seven, and of the independence of the United States of America the twelfth. In witness whereof we have hereunto subscribed our names. [Names omitted]

Articles in addition to, and amendment of, the Constitution of the United States of America, proposed by Congress, and ratified by the legislatures of the several States pursuant to the fifth article of the original Constitution.

AMENDMENTS

First Ten Amendments passed by Congress Sept. 25, 1789.
Ratified by three-fourths of the States December 15, 1791.

ARTICLE I

Congress shall make no law respecting an establishment of religion, or prohibiting the free exercise thereof; or abridging the freedom of speech, or of the press; or the right of the people peaceably to assemble, and to petition the government for a redress of grievances.

ARTICLE II

A well regulated militia, being necessary to the security of a free State, the right of the people to keep and bear arms, shall not be infringed.

ARTICLE III

No soldier shall, in time of peace be quartered in any house, without the consent of the owner, nor in time of war, but in a manner to be prescribed by law.

ARTICLE IV

The right of the people to be secure in their persons, houses, papers, and effects, against unreasonable searches and seizures, shall not be violated, and no warrants shall issue, but upon probable cause, supported by oath or affirmation, and particularly describing the place to be searched, and the persons or things to be seized.

ARTICLE V

No person shall be held to answer for a capital, or otherwise infamous crime, unless on a presentment or indictment of a grand jury, except in cases arising in the land or naval forces, or in the militia, when in actual service in time of war or public danger; nor shall any person be subject for the same offense to be twice put in jeopardy of life or limb; nor shall be compelled in any criminal case to be a witness against himself, nor be deprived of life, liberty, or property, without due process of law; nor shall private property be taken for public use without just compensation.

ARTICLE VI

In all criminal prosecutions, the accused shall enjoy the right to a speedy and public trial, by an impartial jury of the State and district wherein the crime shall have been committed, which district shall have been previously ascertained by law, and to be informed of the nature and cause of the accusation; to be confronted with the witnesses against him; to have compulsory process for obtaining witnesses in his favor, and to have the assistance of counsel for his defense.

ARTICLE VII

In suits at common law, where the value in controversy shall exceed twenty dollars, the right of trial by jury shall be preserved, and no fact tried by a jury shall be otherwise reëxamined in any court of the United States, than according to the rules of the common law.

ARTICLE VIII

Excessive bail shall not be required, nor excessive fines imposed, nor cruel and unusual punishments inflicted.

ARTICLE IX

The enumeration in the Constitution of certain rights shall not be construed to deny or disparage others retained by the people.

ARTICLE X

The powers not delegated to the United States by the Constitution, nor prohibited by it to the States, are reserved to the States respectively, or to the people.

ARTICLE XI

Passed by Congress March 4, 1794. Ratified February 7, 1795.

The judicial power of the United States shall not be construed to extend to any suit in law or equity, commenced or prosecuted against one of the United States by citizens of another State, or by citizens or subjects of any foreign State.

ARTICLE XII

Passed by Congress December 9, 1803. Ratified July 27, 1804.

The electors shall meet in their respective States, and vote by ballot for President and Vice President, one of whom, at least, shall not be an inhabitant of the same State with themselves; they shall name in their ballots the person voted for as President, and in distinct ballots, the person voted for as Vice President, and they shall make distinct lists of all persons voted for as President and of all persons voted for as Vice President, and of the number of votes for each, which lists they shall sign and certify, and transmit sealed to the seat of the government of the United States, directed to the President of the Senate;—The President of the Senate shall, in the presence of the Senate and House of Representatives, open all the certificates and the votes shall then be counted;—The person having the greatest number of votes for President, shall be the President, if such number be a majority of the whole number of electors appointed; and if no person have such majority, then from the persons having the highest numbers not exceeding three on the list of those voted for as President, the House of Representatives shall choose immediately, by ballot, the President. But in choosing the President, the votes shall be taken by States, the representation from each State having one vote; a quorum for this purpose shall consist of a member or members from two thirds of the States, and a majority of all the States shall be necessary to a choice. And if the House of Representatives shall not choose a President whenever the right of choice shall devolve upon them, before the fourth day of March* next following, then the Vice President shall act as President, as in the case of the death or other constitutional disability of the President. The person having the greatest number of votes as Vice President shall be the Vice President, if such number be a majority of the whole number of electors appointed, and if no person have a majority, then from the two highest numbers on the list, the Senate shall choose the Vice President; a quorum for the purpose shall consist of two thirds of the whole number of Senators, and a majority of the whole number shall be necessary to a choice. But no person constitutionally ineligible to the office of President shall be eligible to that of Vice President of the United States.

ARTICLE XIII

Passed by Congress January 31, 1865. Ratified December 6, 1865.

SECTION 1. Neither slavery nor involuntary servitude, except as punishment for crime whereof the party shall have been duly convicted,

* See 20th Amendment.

shall exist within the United States, or any place subject to their jurisdiction.

SECTION 2.   Congress shall have power to enforce this article by appropriate legislation.

ARTICLE XIV

Passed by Congress June 13, 1866. Ratified July 9, 1868.

SECTION 1.   All persons born or naturalized in the United States, and subject to the jurisdiction thereof, are citizens of the United States and of the State wherein they reside. No State shall make or enforce any law which shall abridge the privileges or immunities of citizens of the United States; nor shall any State deprive any person of life, liberty, or property, without due process of law; nor deny to any person within its jurisdiction the equal protection of the laws.

SECTION 2.   Representatives shall be apportioned among the several States according to their respective numbers, counting the whole number of persons in each State, excluding Indians not taxed. But when the right to vote at any election for the choice of electors for President and Vice President of the United States, representatives in Congress, the executive and judicial officers of a State, or the members of the legislature thereof, is denied to any of the male inhabitants of such State, being twenty-one years of age, and citizens of the United States, or in any way abridged, except for participation in rebellion, or other crime, the basis of representation therein shall be reduced in the proportion which the number of such male citizens shall bear to the whole number of male citizens twenty-one years of age in such State.

SECTION 3.   No person shall be a senator or representative in Congress, or elector of President and Vice President, or hold any office, civil or military, under the United States, or under any State, who having previously taken an oath, as a member of Congress, or as an officer of the United States, or as a member of any State legislature, or as an executive or judicial officer of any State, to support the Constitution of the United States, shall have engaged in insurrection or rebellion against the same, or given aid or comfort to the enemies thereof. But Congress may by a vote of two thirds of each House, remove such disability.

SECTION 4.   The validity of the public debt of the United States, authorized by law, including debts incurred for payment of pensions and bounties for services in suppressing insurrection or rebellion, shall not be questioned. But neither the United States nor any State shall assume or pay any debt or obligation incurred in aid of insurrection or rebellion against the United States, or any claim for the loss or emancipation of any slave; but all such debts, obligations, and claims shall be held illegal and void.

SECTION 5. The Congress shall have power to enforce, by appropriate legislation, the provisions of this article.

ARTICLE XV

Passed by Congress February 26, 1869. Ratified February 3, 1870.

SECTION 1. The right of citizens of the United States to vote shall not be denied or abridged by the United States or by any State on account of race, color, or previous condition of servitude.

SECTION 2. The Congress shall have power to enforce this article by appropriate legislation.

ARTICLE XVI

Passed by Congress July 2, 1909. Ratified February 3, 1913.

The Congress shall have power to lay and collect taxes on incomes, from whatever source derived, without apportionment among the several States, and without regard to any census or enumeration.

ARTICLE XVII

Passed by Congress May 13, 1912. Ratified April 8, 1913.

The Senate of the United States shall be composed of two senators from each state, elected by the people thereof, for six years; and each senator shall have one vote. The electors in each State shall have the qualifications requisite for electors of the most numerous branch of the State legislature.

When vacancies happen in the representation of any State in the Senate, the executive authority of such State shall issue writs of election to fill such vacancies: *Provided,* That the legislature of any State may empower the executive thereof to make temporary appointments until the people fill the vacancies by election as the legislature may direct.

This amendment shall not be so construed as to affect the election or term of any senator chosen before it becomes valid as part of the Constitution.

ARTICLE XVIII*

Passed by Congress December 18, 1917. Ratified January 16, 1919.

After one year from the ratification of this article, the manufacture, sale, or transportation of intoxicating liquors within, the importation thereof into, or the exportation thereof from the United States and all territory subject to the jurisdiction thereof for beverage purposes is hereby prohibited.

The Congress and the several States shall have concurrent power to enforce this article by appropriate legislation.

This article shall be inoperative unless it shall have been ratified as an amendment to the Constitution by the legislatures of the several States, as provided in the Constitution, within seven years from the date of the submission hereof to the states by Congress.

ARTICLE XIX

Passed by Congress June 4, 1919. Ratified August 18, 1920.

The right of citizens of the United States to vote shall not be denied or abridged by the United States or by any State on account of sex.

The Congress shall have power by appropriate legislation to enforce the provisions of this article.

ARTICLE XX

Passed by Congress March 2, 1932. Ratified January 23, 1933.

SECTION 1.   The terms of the President and Vice President shall end at noon on the 20th day of January, and the terms of Senators and Representatives at noon on the 3d day of January, of the years in which such terms would have ended if this article had not been ratified; and the terms of their successors shall then begin.

* Repealed by the 21st Amendment.

SECTION 2. The Congress shall assemble at least once in every year, and such meeting shall begin at noon on the 3d day of January, unless they shall by law appoint a different day.

SECTION 3. If, at the time fixed for the beginning of the term of the President, the President-elect shall have died, the Vice President-elect shall become President. If a President shall not have been chosen before the time fixed for the beginning of his term, or if the President-elect shall have failed to qualify, then the Vice President-elect shall act as President until a President shall have qualified; and the Congress may by law provide for the case wherein neither a President-elect nor a Vice President-elect shall have qualified, declaring who shall then act as President, or the manner in which one who is to act shall be selected, and such person shall act accordingly until a President or Vice President shall have qualified.

SECTION 4. The Congress may by law provide for the case of the death of any of the persons from whom the House of Representatives may choose a President whenever the right of choice shall have devolved upon them, and for the case of the death of any of the persons from whom the Senate may choose a Vice President whenever the right of choice shall have devolved upon them.

SECTION 5. Sections 1 and 2 shall take effect on the 15th day of October following the ratification of this article.

SECTION 6. This article shall be inoperative unless it shall have been ratified as an amendment to the Constitution by the legislatures of three-fourths of the several States within seven years from the date of its submission.

ARTICLE XXI

Passed by Congress February 20, 1933. Ratified December 5, 1933.

SECTION 1. The Eighteenth Article of amendment to the Constitution of the United States is hereby repealed.

SECTION 2. The transportation or importation into any State, Territory, or possession of the United States for delivery or use therein of intoxicating liquors in violation of the laws thereof, is hereby prohibited.

SECTION 3. This article shall be inoperative unless it shall have been ratified as an amendment to the Constitution by conventions in the several States, as provided in the Constitution, within seven years from the date of the submission thereof to the States by the Congress.

ARTICLE XXII

Passed by Congress March 21, 1947. Ratified February 27, 1951.

No person shall be elected to the office of the President more than twice, and no person who has held the office of President, or acted as President, for more than two years of a term to which some other person was elected President shall be elected to the office of the President more than once.

But this article shall not apply to any person holding the office of President when this article was proposed by the Congress, and shall not prevent any person who may be holding the office of President, or acting as President, during the term within which this article becomes operative from holding the office of President or acting as President during the remainder of such term.

This article shall be inoperative unless it shall have been ratified as an amendment to the Constitution by the legislatures of three-fourths of the several states within seven years from the date of its submission to the states by the Congress.

ARTICLE XXIII

Passed by Congress June 16, 1960. Ratified March 29, 1961.

SECTION 1. The District constituting the seat of Government of the United States shall appoint in such manner as the Congress may direct:

A number of electors of President and Vice President equal to the whole number of Senators and Representatives in Congress to which the District would be entitled if it were a State, but in no event more than the least populous state; they shall be in addition to those appointed by the states, but shall be considered, for the purpose of the election of President and Vice President, to be electors appointed by a state; and they shall meet in the District and perform such duties as provided by the twelfth article of amendment.

SECTION 2. The Congress shall have power to enforce this article by appropriate legislation.

ARTICLE   XXIV

Passed by Congress August 27, 1962. Ratified January 23, 1964.

SECTION 1.   The right of citizens of the United States to vote in any primary or other election for President or Vice President, for electors for President or Vice President, or for Senator or Repesentative in Congress, shall not be denied or abridged by the United States or any State by reason of failure to pay any poll tax or other tax.

SECTION 2.   The Congress shall have the power to enforce this article by appropriate legislation.

ARTICLE XXV

Passed by Congress July 6, 1965. Ratified February 10, 1967.

SECTION 1.   In case of the removal of the President from office or his death or resignation, the Vice President shall become President.

SECTION 2.   Whenever there is a vacancy in the office of the Vice President, the President shall nominate a Vice President who shall take the office upon confirmation by a majority vote of both houses of Congress.

SECTION 3.   Whenever the President transmits to the President pro tempore of the Senate and the Speaker of the House of Representatives his written declaration that he is unable to discharge the powers and duties of his office, and until he transmits to them a written declaration to the contrary, such powers and duties shall be discharged by the Vice President as Acting President.

SECTION 4.   Whenever the Vice President and a majority of either the principal officers of the executive departments, or of such other body as Congress may by law provide, transmit to the President pro tempore of the Senate and the Speaker of the House of Representatives their written declaration that the President is unable to discharge the powers and duties of his office, the Vice President shall immediately assume the powers and duties of the office of Acting President.

Thereafter, when the President transmits to the President pro tempore of the Senate and the Speaker of the House of Representatives his written declaration that no inability exists, he shall resume the powers and duties of his office unless the Vice President and a majority of either the principal officers of the executive department, or of such other body as Congress may by law provide, transmit within four days to the President pro tempore of the Senate and the Speaker of the House of Representatives their written declaration that the President is unable to discharge the powers and duties of his office. Thereupon Congress shall decide the issue, assembling within 48 hours for that purpose if not in session. If the Congress, within 21 days after receipt of the latter written declaration, or, if Congress is not in session, within 21 days after Congress is required to assemble, determines by two-thirds vote of both houses that the President is unable to discharge the powers and duties of his office, the Vice President shall continue to discharge the same as Acting President; otherwise, the President shall resume the powers and duties of his office.

ARTICLE XXVI

Passed by Congress March 23, 1971. Ratified June 30, 1971.

SECTION 1. The right of citizens of the United States, who are eighteen years of age or older, to vote shall not be denied or abridged by the United States or any state on account of age.

SECTION 2. The Congress shall have the power to enforce this article by appropriate legislation.

THE SUPREME COURT
AND THE CONSTITUTION

Chief Justice Hughes once remarked that the Constitution means what the Supreme Court says it means; and Woodrow Wilson said that the Supreme Court resembles a constitutional convention in continuous session. The Supreme Court is very nearly the final interpreter of the Constitution. Its decisions can be overridden by the adoption of a constitutional amendment; but this has happened only four times in widely spaced cases: *Chisholm* v. *Georgia* (1793) by the Eleventh Amendment; *Dred Scott* v. *Sandford* (1857) by the Fourteenth Amendment; *Pollock* v. *Farmers' Loan and Trust Co.* (1895) by the Sixteenth Amendment and *Oregon* v. *Mitchell* (1970) by the Twenty-sixth Amendment.

The Background of Judicial Review. One searches in vain in the Constitution for a statement granting the power of judicial review to the Supreme Court. It is not in Article III among the subjects over which the federal courts have jurisdiction; and in Article VI, it is "The judges in every state" who are bound by the supremacy clause, with no mention of a federal court to review and make uniform the state courts' decisions. In the Convention of 1787 the framers debated at some length the need for an authority, to include some judges as well as the executive, with power to veto legislative acts; but the proposal was voted down. How, then, was it possible for judicial review to become established as one of the most significant features of the American constitutional system?

One of the most important influences was the Anglo-American legal system. The common law of England, which has been called "the fruit of reason ripened by precedent," was built up case by case in decisions by the courts, the latest decision forming a precedent for the decision of similar cases that followed. The common law was brought to America and formed the basis of law in all the colonies. Another predisposing influence was the existence of written charters and other documents granting or limiting the powers of the colonial governments. The English Privy Council could disallow for the King the acts of colonial legislatures and, through its judicial committee, it heard appeals from colonial courts. Theories of Locke and Montesquieu on the desirability of limiting powers of governmental organs, including the legislature, formed another important influence.

In Number 78 of *The Federalist* papers, Alexander Hamilton argued forcefully for judicial review, on the ground that the Constitution is superior to ordinary legislation and can be preserved only through the judiciary's declaring void all legislative acts manifestly in conflict with its provisions. In 1798, Jefferson and Madison advanced a different means of reviewing acts of Congress. Through the Kentucky and Virginia Resolutions they called on the other states to declare whether the Alien and Sedition Acts were, or were not, constitutional. Every state north of Maryland replied, condemning the constitutional principle underlying the Resolutions and most of them declaring that the judiciary is the proper organ to interpret the Constitution.

John Marshall. The Supreme Court's development of judicial review was largely the work of John Marshall, who was appointed Chief Justice by President John Adams just before Jefferson became President and the Republicans took control of Congress. In *Marbury* v. *Madison* (1803), Marshall wrote the opinion declaring unconstitutional a minor provision of the Judiciary Act of 1789, thereby creating a precedent for review of federal legislation. In *Fletcher* v. *Peck* (1810), the Court for the first time declared unconstitutional a state legislative act. Then followed a large number of cases in which federal exercise of power was sustained and state encroachments on the federal sphere were usually invalidated. Among the most important were *McCulloch* v. *Maryland* (1816), in which Marshall exploited the resources of the "necessary and proper clause" of Article I, section 8 to create the doctrine of implied powers; and *Gibbons* v. *Ogden,* in which Marshall's definition of commerce included far more than appeared possible in the brief general wording of the constitutional grant of powers. These cases form significant parts of the law today.

Roger B. Taney. The next Chief Justice, Roger B. Taney, who served from 1836 to 1864, had been President Jackson's Attorney General and reflected Jacksonian attitudes toward states' rights and private property. During his tenure, the Court halted, and in some respects reversed, its trend toward centralization. By referring to the

Tenth Amendment, Taney sought to carve out separate spheres for the states and the federal government. He was less concerned than Marshall had been with supporting the status quo. His most famous—or notorious—decision was that of *Dred Scott* v. *Sandford,* in which he attempted to settle the slavery controversy (and in which, by declaring the Missouri Compromise unconstitutional, he confirmed the precedent for judicial review set in *Marbury* v. *Madison*).

The Post-Civil War Court. During the Civil War, the Supreme Court lost prestige because military considerations often overrode judicial determinations of constitutional rights. During the Reconstruction period, the Court found itself in the middle of the constitutional struggle between the Radicals, who controlled Congress, and President Andrew Johnson. The Court's structure and jurisdiction were manipulated for partisan purposes. Though it was more active than ever before in declaring state and federal laws unconstitutional, the trend of its decisions was uncertain. None of the Chief Justices possessed the dominating qualities of leadership that had made Marshall and Taney great. There were some Associate Justices of first-rate ability, including Miller, Field, and Harlan, but they were in a minority among others who had been attorneys for business interests and who carried onto the Court their bias in favor of *laissez faire.* The demands of Greenbackers and Populists for social reforms affected the Court scarcely at all. Before the end of the nineteenth century it had invalidated federal income taxes, defined the word "commerce" so as to prevent the full enforcement of the Sherman Antitrust Act, and washed its hands of the racial problem.

The Early Twentieth-Century Court. After the beginning of the twentieth century, the Court permitted a limited enforcement of the antitrust acts, but it demonstrated its partiality toward business by developing two dogmas of constitutional construction that later courts have discredited. Under "freedom of contract," the Court invalidated state and federal attempts to regulate wages and hours of work on the ground that they violated an individual's right to contract with his employer for the sale of his labor. Under "business affected with a public interest," it struck down legislative regulations of businesses other than those (e.g., an inn or a public utility) which had traditionally been subject to public regulation. In its interpretation of the commerce and taxing powers, the Court upheld laws for the benefit of business and agriculture, but was strangely unable to find a constitutional basis for child labor legislation. (Compare *McCray* v. *United States* with *Bailey*

v. *Drexel Furniture Co.*) Able and forward-looking justices like Holmes and Brandeis protested against such interpretations and, by their dissenting opinions, prepared the way for a new direction in constitutional law.

The New Deal Revolution. During the depression of the 1930s, President Franklin D. Roosevelt proposed, and Congress enacted, bold new legislation regulating many phases of American industry. It was inevitable that such legislation would be brought before the Supreme Court for review. The Court was then nearly equally divided. Four Justices, Van Devanter, McReynolds, Sutherland, and Butler, were in favor of continuing the recent precedents of the Court. Three Justices, Brandeis, Stone, and Cardozo, believed that the Constitution should be interpreted in the light of existing economic conditions, and were unwilling in matters of policy to substitute their own opinions for those of the legislature. Chief Justice Hughes usually sided with these three. Associate Justice Roberts at first was usually on the side of the four conservatives and with them made up a majority that declared unconstitutional most of the early New Deal legislation. After the Democratic landslide in the election of 1936, President Roosevelt proposed to add to the Court's membership one new Justice for each of the sitting Justices over seventy years of age on the ground that the aged Justices could not keep up with their work. Thereupon, the sequence of events was as follows: The Chief Justice presented proof that the Court's calendar was up to date. Congress was unwilling to accept the President's "court-packing" plan. Justice Roberts switched to the liberal point of view, and the Court began to uphold the more carefully considered and better drafted measures that Congress passed to replace those that the Court had invalidated. In the process, the meaning of interstate commerce was expanded to include all but purely local production and trade. *Intrastate* commerce and the Tenth Amendment lost nearly all significance in constitutional law.

The Warren Court. The appointment of Earl Warren as Chief Justice in 1953 was an event of special significance. Though Warren did not dominate the Court in the manner of Marshall or Taney, he exercised a steady and consistent influence as one of a small liberal majority. His most famous decision was *Brown* v. *Board of Education of Topeka,* in which for a unanimous Court he announced that the mere fact of racial segregation in public schools was a violation of the Fourteenth Amendment. During his sixteen-year tenure, the Court made the Bill of Rights more explicit than ever before. In numerous cases it expanded the meaning of freedom of speech and press, invalidated state laws tending toward an establishment of religion, brought nearly all the procedural guarantees in the Fourth through the Eighth Amendments within the protection of the Fourteenth Amendment, and restored equality among the constituencies from which, respectively, members of the House of Representatives and the two houses of the state legislatures are elected. The Warren Court has been termed "activist" because it was not content to decide cases on the basis of time-honored precedents, but boldly created new precedents to protect the rights of individuals.

How Cases Reach the Supreme Court. Nowadays only suits between states come to the Court on original jurisdiction. Most cases are heard under the Court's appellate jurisdiction after they have been decided either by a lower federal court (usually a Court of Appeals) or by the highest state court having jurisdiction to try the particular case. The right to appeal is strictly limited. Congress has required that the Supreme Court rule finally on all cases in which a lower federal court has found any federal or state law unconstitutional or in which a state court has upheld a state law against the claim that it violated the Constitution, a federal law, or a treaty.

Other cases come to the Supreme Court on writ of certiorari, which Congress has authorized since 1925. A disappointed litigant may petition the Court for the writ, and if four Justices approve, the case comes before the Court. The usual grounds for granting a petition for the writ are that the case presents a fundamental constitutional issue, or is of general importance, or concerns an important private right, or involves the interpretation of a statute that has not previously been presented to the Court; or that decisions of different lower courts on the subject have varied and need to be brought into conformity. Through its power to grant or withhold certiorari the Court can determine within limits the cases that will come before it.

How the Court Operates. The Justices examine the record of the case in the lower court, study the briefs of counsel, and hear oral arguments. The outcome is determined by a majority vote of the Justices; if there is no majority the decision of the lower court stands. Usually the Chief Justice assigns the writing of the Court's opinions among the Justices who have voted with the majority, himself taking his turn. If the Chief Justice is in the minority, the senior Associate Justice who voted with the majority makes the assignment. A Justice who disagrees with the decision of the Court may write a dissenting opinion. If a Justice agrees with the decision, but not with the reasons given in the opinion of the Court, he may write a concurring opinion. Such opinions, especially dissents, sometimes foreshadow changing interpretations of constitutional law.

Effect of Precedents. Precedents set by the Supreme Court are binding on all lower courts, state and federal. The Supreme Court is not obliged to follow its own precedents, but it usually does so. Frequent reversals of precedents would make the law uncertain and the outcome of later cases unpredictable. On the other hand, excessive devotion to a line of precedents creates the unfortunate situation where the law is out of tune with the realities of a changing society. The Court has several choices. It may on narrow grounds distinguish the case before it from earlier cases and apply a different ruling. It may specifically overrule the precedent. It may ignore the precedent, in effect overruling it *sub silentio*. It may call the issue of the case a political question to be decided by Congress or the President. Whatever it does, the latest decision of the Court becomes part of the body of constitutional law.

SELECTED CASES

*Following is a selection of cases that are landmarks in the develop-
ment of the Constitution by judicial interpretation. Somewhat more than
half the cases are related to the federal system and the powers of the
federal government. The others show the Supreme Court's concern with
the protection of private rights. With few exceptions, the topical
arrangement of cases follows the order of the Constitution. Under each
topic the cases are arranged in chronological order so that the reader
may follow the evolution of some basic constitutional principles and
the abandonment of other doctrines previously upheld as constitutional.*

JUDICIAL REVIEW

Marbury v. Madison (1803). The first elaboration by the Court of
the principle of judicial review. William Marbury applied directly
to the Supreme Court, as provided by the Judiciary Act of 1789,
for a writ of mandamus to compel Secretary of State James Madison
to deliver a commission which had been signed and sealed by the
previous Secretary of State. The Court through Chief Justice Marshall
declared that under Article III, section 2, of the Constitution it
could issue a writ of mandamus only when exercising appellate
jurisdiction; hence the provision of the Judiciary Act authorizing the
writ of mandamus in original jurisdiction, on which Marbury had
relied, was void. The Constitution, said the Court, is the fundamental
law; and in cases of conflict between it and a statute, "an Act of the
Legislature repugnant to the Constitution is void. . . . It is emphatically the province and duty of the judicial department to say what
the law is."

Fletcher v. Peck (1810). The case in which a state law was first declared unconstitutional. It grew out of an attempt of the legislature of Georgia in 1796 to repeal a huge grant of land made corruptly by the previous legislature, the members of which had been bribed by speculators (the Yazoo Land Fraud). The Court held (*a*) that the action of one legislature in rescinding the grant made by another was void because, although legislative acts may be repealed, rights vested under prior acts cannot be divested, and (*b*) that the original grant was in the nature of a contract, the obligation of which, under Article I, section 10 of the Constitution, cannot be impaired.

Martin v. Hunter's Lessee (**1816**). *See under* Jurisdiction of the Federal Courts, page 98.

THE PROCESS OF AMENDMENT

Hawke v. Smith (1920). The Court held that a popular referendum authorized by a state constitution may not undo the state legislature's ratification of an amendment to the Constitution of the United States, when, according to Article V, the legislature is designated by Congress as the ratifying body. When it acts in this capacity, it is subject to the Constitution of the United States and not to the constitution of the state.

Coleman v. Miller (1939). This case grew out of the Kansas legislature's belated ratification of the proposed child labor amendment which had been submitted by Congress in 1924. The Court held that Congress, and not the courts, has power to determine the validity of ratifications by the states; that the time permitted the states for ratification is to be determined by Congress; and that a proposed amendment must be presumed to be still pending until Congress rules otherwise. (Congressional precedents hold that a state legislature may ratify an amendment after a previous rejection; a legislature may not rescind a ratification once it has been reported to the proper federal authority as having been made; and Congress, in proposing an amendment, may set a time limit for ratification, after which the proposed amendment becomes inoperative.)

IMPLIED POWERS

McCulloch v. Maryland (1819). The classic exposition of the doctrine of implied powers. The case arose from the refusal of the cashier of the Baltimore branch of the Bank of the United States to pay a tax levied by Maryland on the issuance of notes by the branch. Chief Justice Marshall, for the Court, declared that, contrary to the contention of counsel for Maryland, the last clause of Article I, section 8, does not limit Congress to the enactment of laws but, on the contrary, gives Congress means to carry out its expressly granted powers; and that the Bank was "necessary and proper" to taxing, borrowing, and conveying funds for the support of armies. "Let the end be legitimate, let it be within the scope of the Constitution, and all means which are appropriate, which are plainly adapted to that end, which are not prohibited, but consist with the letter and spirit of the Constitution, are constitutional." And Maryland could not tax the Bank because such a use of the state's taxing power threatens the supremacy of the federal government in matters committed to its jurisdiction. "The States have no power, by taxation or otherwise, to retard, impede, burden, or in any manner control, the operation of the constitutional laws enacted by Congress to carry into execution the powers vested in the general government."

SUPREMACY OF FEDERAL LAW

United States v. Peters (1809). The Court held that the legislature of Pennsylvania could not, by declaring that the decision of a lower United States court was in violation of the Eleventh Amendment, impede the execution of the laws of the United States.

Ableman v. Booth (1859). The Court held that a Wisconsin court could not, by a writ of habeas corpus, effect the release of a prisoner who was in custody of a United States marshal for having violated federal law by helping a fugitive slave to escape. When a person is legally in federal custody for a federal offense and this fact has been made known to state authorities by proper return on a writ of habeas corpus, the state may not proceed further because federal authority is exclusive.

Pennsylvania v. Nelson (1956). Reversed a conviction under a state sedition law on the grounds (*a*) that Congress, in passing the Smith Act, and other acts, had evinced an intention to occupy or reoccupy the field of antiseditious legislation; (*b*) that the federal interest is dominant and pervasive; and (*c*) that a state program in this area might conflict with federal aims.

THE PLACE OF THE STATES IN THE NATION

Texas v. White (1869). The Court held that secession was not constitutionally possible. After the Civil War the Governor of Texas sued to recover possession of United States bonds (acquired in 1850) that had been sold on the order of the secessionist legislature to purchase supplies for the Confederate army. The Court held that Texas was entitled to recover the bonds. When she entered the Union, she entered into an indissoluble relationship. Hence her ordinance of secession and all acts of her legislature intended to give effect to it were absolutely void. "The Constitution, in all its provisions, looks to an indestructible Union composed of indestructible States."

Stearns v. Minnesota (1900). The Court held that restrictions on state taxation of public lands imposed by Congress when granting lands to Minnesota at the time of her admission could be enforced, because the provision did not impair Minnesota's sovereignty or her legal equality with other states.

Coyle v. Smith (1911). Upheld the right of Oklahoma to change the location of her capital, contrary to a condition imposed by Congress when Oklahoma was admitted. The Court held that the location of the capital is a matter of state policy for state authorities to determine. And when admitted, Oklahoma became legally equal to every other state.

FEDERAL GUARANTEES TO STATES

Luther v. Borden (1849). The first Court elaboration of the doctrine of "political questions." The case arose after the Dorr Rebellion in 1841, during which two rival governments existed in Rhode Island: one was regularly elected and based on a long-standing property qualification for voting, the other (Dorr's) based on an informal election with manhood suffrage. On request of the older government, President Tyler ordered militia into the state and Dorr's government collapsed. In construing Article IV, section 4, of the Constitution, the Court declined to say which government was republican in form or whether or not on this occasion the President had been justified in acting to suppress domestic disorders. The Court declared that these were political questions to be resolved as they arose by Congress and the President.

Pacific States Telephone and Telegraph Co. v. Oregon (1912). Declared that the clause in Article IV, section 4, guaranteeing a republican form of government is nonjusticiable. The company had asked the Court to invalidate a tax that had been imposed by the state after proposal and enactment by popular initiative, contending that the initiative had made the government unrepresentative and therefore unrepublican. The Court held that the case presented a political question to be resolved by Congress when admitting Senators and Representatives from the state.

FULL FAITH AND CREDIT

Atherton v. Atherton (1901). The Court held that when husband and wife are domiciled in different states, a divorce decree granted in one state must be given full faith and credit in the other, even though the out-of-state spouse has not been given personal notice of the proceedings.

Haddock v. Haddock (1906). The Court held that the state of the marriage domicile (New York) need not give full faith and credit when the husband had moved his residence to another state (Connecticut) and there had obtained a decree of divorce without giving his wife, who had continued to reside in New York, personal notice of the suit. But, the Court said, the decree was valid in Connecticut, because a state has the right to determine the marital status of its citizens.

Williams v. North Carolina (1942, 1945). Overruled *Haddock* v. *Haddock*. A husband living in North Carolina and his next-door neighbor's wife went to Nevada, lived for six weeks (the minimum period required by Nevada law) in a trailer camp, obtained divorces from their respective spouses, and were married to each other. Upon their return to North Carolina, they were convicted of bigamy. The Supreme Court ruled that divorces obtained after changing domiciles are valid and must be given full faith and credit in other states. North Carolina again challenged the divorce, alleging that Williams's residence in Nevada had not been acquired in good faith. The Court held in 1945 that the courts of the state of the original marriage domicile could determine the jurisdictional fact whether or not a party to a divorce had acquired a legal domicile in another state, and if bad faith were conclusively proved there, the state could disregard the divorce decree.

Sherrer v. Sherrer (1948). The Court held that in a contested divorce proceeding, when both parties are present or represented by counsel, the determination of domicile by a state court must be recognized in other states.

SUFFRAGE AND ELECTIONS

Ex Parte Siebold (1880). Let stand the conviction in a federal court of a state-appointed election commissioner for violating both state and federal laws by stuffing the ballot box. The Court said that under Article I, section 4, Congress has plenary and paramount jurisdiction over the election of Congressmen, and that its power extends to supervision of state election regulations "so as to give every citizen his free right to vote without molestation or injury."

Guinn v. United States (1915). Declared void an amendment to the constitution of Oklahoma which contained a "grandfather clause" requiring a literacy test for all voters in state and national elections except those who, under any form of government, were entitled to vote on January 1, 1866, or who then resided in some foreign nation, or who were the lineal descendants of such persons. The Court said that, though race, color, and previous servitude were not mentioned, the selection of a date prior to the adoption of the Fifteenth Amendment was obviously intended to disfranchise Negro residents "in direct and positive disregard" of that Amendment.

Harper v. Virginia State Board of Elections (1966). The decision which, after the adoption of the Twenty-fourth Amendment, gave the final blow to the poll-tax requirement. The Court declared unconstitutional a state law requiring payment of a poll tax as a prerequisite for voting in state and local elections, because wealth and tax-paying have no relation to ability to exercise the suffrage, and because the imposition of a fee, however small, discriminates arbitrarily and hence violates the equal-protection clause of the Fourteenth Amendment.

South Carolina v. Katzenbach (1966). Upheld provisions of the Federal Voting Rights Act of 1965 which (*a*) prohibited subterfuges to evade the Fifteenth Amendment, specifically requirements for tests and devices of literacy, educational attainment, moral character, or voucher by registered voters; and which (*b*) provided for federal officers to register voters in states or their subdivisions where less than 50 percent of the adult population were registered or voted in the election of 1964. The Court declared that "as against the reserved powers of the states, Congress may use any rational means to effect the constitutional prohibition of racial discrimination in voting."

Oregon v. Mitchell (1970). Upheld the constitutionality of a 1970 amendment to the Voting Rights Act lowering the minimum voting age to eighteen in elections for the President and members of Congress but declared the provision unconstitutional in elections for state and local offices. Justice Black, who wrote the opinion, said that the right of Congress to regulate the suffrage was implied from Article I, section 4, "which was part of the plan of the Founding Fathers to insure that the government under the Constitution would survive." After the decision Congress submitted, and the state legislatures adopted the Twenty-sixth Amendment to the Constitution, extending the suffrage to eighteen-year-olds in all elections.

PRIMARY ELECTIONS

Newberry v. United States (1921). Reversed the conviction of Truman H. Newberry for violating the federal Corrupt Practices Act of 1910 by spending an excessive amount in his successful campaign against Henry Ford for the Republican nomination for United States Senator from Michigan. The Court held that a primary is in no real sense a part of an election.

United States v. Classic (1941). Let stand the conviction of a Louisiana election officer who perpetrated frauds in a primary election in which a member of Congress was nominated. The Court cited *Ex parte Siebold* as to the voter's right to participate in the general election and declared: "Where the state law has made the primary an integral part of the procedure of choice, or where in fact the primary effectively controls the choice, the right of the elector to have his ballot counted at the primary is likewise included in the right protected by Article I, section 2."

Texas Primary Cases (1927–1953). In *Nixon v. Herndon* (1927), the Court invalidated a law of the Texas legislature which excluded Negroes from primary elections of the Democratic party on the ground that it deprived them of rights under the equal-protection clause of the Fourteenth Amendment. A new law giving the executive committee of the party the power to determine eligibility of primary voters met a like fate in *Nixon v. Condon* (1932), which held that when the committee excluded Negroes, it acted as an agent of the state. But when the party convention excluded Negroes, the Court declined to interfere in *Grovey* v. *Townsend* (1935) on the ground that under Texas laws a political party was a private organization. After *United States* v. *Classic* had declared primaries part of the election process, the Court overruled *Grovey* v. *Townsend* and, in *Smith* v. *Allwright* (1944), held that the right of Negroes to vote in primary elections could not be nullified by a state through casting its election laws in a form which permitted a political party to practice discrimination. In *Terry* v. *Adams* (1953), the Court outlawed the all-white Jaybird organization primaries held before the regular Democratic primaries which for many years controlled the party's nominations (and hence in a Texas county the results of general elections).

LEGISLATIVE DISTRICTING

Colegrove v. Green (1946). The Court declared that a suit to compel a reapportionment presented a political question. Though the rural-dominated legislature of Illinois had not changed the boundaries of congressional districts in the state since 1901, and though great discrepancies in population existed among the districts, the Court declined to intervene because (*a*) the Court ought not to become involved in partisan politics; (*b*) it could not itself redistrict the state; and (*c*) authority for dealing with such problems was vested by the Constitution (Article I, section 4) in Congress.

Baker v. Carr (1962). Invalidated a Tennessee legislative apportionment of 1901 which had remained unaltered despite losses of population in many counties and large increases in others. Rejecting the rule of *Colegrove* v. *Green,* the Court held that the equitable apportionment of voters among districts from which members of the state legislature are chosen is a justiciable, and not a political question; and that, when the apportionment is determined to be inequitable, the courts can provide relief.

Wesberry v. Sanders (1964). Overruled *Colegrove* v. *Green.* Invalidated the unequal apportionment of congressional districts in Georgia on the ground that, since every voter is equal to every other voter, the districts from which representatives in Congress are chosen must be as nearly equal as practicable in population.

Reynolds v. Sims (1964). Extended the principle of "one man, one vote," so as to invalidate the unequal apportionment of seats in both houses of a state (the Alabama) legislature. The Court advised against creating districts with mathematically equal populations because this would be an invitation to partisan gerrymandering and suggested following the boundaries of political subdivisions in creating districts.

Kirkpatrick v. Preisler (1969). The Court held that in dividing a state into congressional districts, the state legislature must make all districts equal in population, or justify the variance or show that it is unavoidable.

LEGISLATIVE PRIVILEGE

Bond v. Floyd (1966). The Court held that the lower house of the Georgia legislature had violated Julian Bond's constitutional right to freedom of speech when it refused to admit him as a member because of his utterances in opposition to the war in Vietnam—for which under the First Amendment he could not have been prosecuted.

Powell v. McCormack (1969). The Court held that the House of Representatives may not add to the constitutional qualifications of age, residence, and citizenship or exclude, by a majority vote, a duly elected member who possesses them. (Adam Clayton Powell had been denied his seat because of charges that in previous Congresses he had submitted false expense accounts and had misused committee funds.) The inhabitants of a congressional district are entitled to representation, and this right can be overridden only by the right of the House to expel a member, which requires a two-thirds vote.

Gravel v. United States (1972). The Court held, five to four, that the legislative aide of a member of Congress shares the member's immunity from being "questioned in any other place" than in the legislative chamber or in committee. But when arrangements are made for *private* publication (as of the "Pentagon Papers," read in committee by Senator Gravel), the aide must tell a grand jury what he knows about how allegedly stolen documents came into the possession of a member of Congress.

INVESTIGATIVE POWERS OF CONGRESS

Kilbourn v. Thompson (1881). The Court held that the investigative powers of Congress are limited to matters within its proper sphere, on which it has shown an intent to legislate. It has no general authority to inquire into other matters.

McGrain v. Daugherty (1927). The Court held that the Senate had acted within its proper powers when it cited for contempt the brother of the Attorney General for refusing to testify before a committee investigating the functioning of the Attorney General's office during the Harding Administration. The investigating power is "an essential and appropriate auxiliary to the legislative function," and legislation for the reform of the Attorney General's office was plainly possible and would be aided by the committee's investigation.

Watkins v. United States (1957). Reversed the conviction of a labor leader who, when called before the House Committee on Un-American Activities, answered freely the questions concerning his own connection with the Communist party but refused to name other persons who he thought had long ago ceased to have any connection with the party. The Court held that when Congress creates a committee it must spell out the jurisdiction of the committee so that the witness and reviewing authorities can determine whether the questions are pertinent. "Investigations conducted solely for the personal aggrandizement of the investigators, or to 'punish' those investigated are indefensible. . . . The Bill of Rights is applicable to all investigations . . . ," but a certain weight "must be ascribed to the interest of Congress in demanding disclosures."

Barenblatt v. United States (1959). The Court held, by a five-to-four vote, that the freedom of speech of a college teacher, or academic freedom, under the First Amendment properly appertained to the classroom and did not protect him from the consequences of refusing to answer pertinent questions about his knowledge of Communist influence and his association with Communists on American college campuses when such questions were asked under the undoubted power of Congress to inquire into alleged Communist infiltration into the field of education.

THE TAXING POWER

McCulloch v. Maryland (1819). *See under* Implied Powers, page 66.

Collector v. Day (1870). Held that the salary of a state judicial officer was exempt from the Civil War income tax levied by Congress. The Court said that if the instrumentalities of the federal government were exempt from state taxation (see *McCulloch* v. *Maryland*), then the instrumentalities of the states, depending on their reserved powers for self-preservation, were equally exempt from federal taxation.

Pollock v. Farmers' Loan and Trust Co. (1894, 1895). Declared unconstitutional an Act of Congress of 1894 that imposed an income tax without apportionment among the states (*see* Article I, section 9), on the ground that a tax on land is a direct tax, and a tax on the income from land is indistinguishable from a tax on the land itself. In 1895, the Court extended the same principle to the income from stocks and bonds. (The Sixteenth Amendment canceled both decisions.)

Knowlton v. Moore (1900). Upheld a tax levied by Congress in 1898 on inheritances of more than $10,000 at rates graduated according to the relationship of the beneficiary to the deceased and the amount of the inheritance. The Court held (*a*) that the tax was not a direct tax on the property transferred but an excise tax on the privilege of transmitting property from the dead to the living and, therefore, was not required to be apportioned among the states; and (*b*) that the constitutional requirement of uniformity means geographical uniformity throughout the United States, not equal treatment for every inheritor of property, and therefore the tax might be levied at progressive rates.

McCray v. United States (1904). The Court refused to inquire into the motives of Congress imposing a tax of ten cents per pound on oleomargarine artificially colored to imitate butter and only 1/4 cent per pound on uncolored oleomargarine. Opponents claimed that the act invaded the sphere of the states, was regulative and not fiscal, and destroyed property rights without due process. The court said that the act was, "on its face," a measure for raising revenue.

South Carolina v. United States (1905). The Court held that liquor dispensaries owned and operated by South Carolina were subject to federal excise taxes because the dispensaries were essentially business enterprises and not instrumentalities of government.

Bailey v. Drexel Furniture Co. (1922). Declared unconstitutional an Act of Congress imposing a tax of 10 per cent on the net profits of any establishment knowingly employing minors under certain ages. The Court held (*a*) that the word "knowingly" applied to criminal law, not to taxation; and (*b*) that the tax was not a bona fide revenue measure but a police regulation, which by invading the sphere of the states, violated the Tenth Amendment.

Helvering v. Gerhardt (1938). The Court held that employees of the Port of New York Authority, which is jointly owned and operated by New York and New Jersey, were liable to federal income taxes. The Court said that such taxes on employees could not obstruct the performance of state functions, and if immunity were granted, "it would restrict the federal taxing power without affording any corresponding tangible protection to the state government."

Graves v. New York ex rel. O'Keefe (1939). Upheld the application of the New York State income tax law to the salary of employees of the Home Owners' Loan Corporation, an agency of the federal government. The Court thus abandoned the rule, derived from *McCulloch* v. *Maryland,* that the salary of federal employees is immune from state taxation.

United States v. Butler (1936). The Court invalidated the first Agricultural Adjustment Act, declaring that the act's coercive federal regulation of farm production and prices invaded the reserved powers of the states; that the processing taxes, levied under the act, were not bona fide taxes but an integral part of an unconstitutional program of regulation and hence themselves invalid; and that, in any case, the taxes, the proceeds of which were to subsidize farmers, could not be sustained under the general-welfare clause of the Constitution. Compare *Mulford* v. *Smith,* page 83.

THE SPENDING POWER

Green v. Frazier (1920). Recognized the right of North Dakota to operate grain elevators, banks, and other business establishments that had the sanction of the state's courts, legislature, and people. The Court held that taxes levied for this program were not to be construed as for a nonpublic purpose.

Massachusetts v. Mellon (1923). Denied the application of Massachusetts for an injunction to prevent the Secretary of the Treasury from disbursing funds under a federal grant to the states for maternal welfare. Massachusetts had claimed that she was coerced to accept the grant or lose her share of federal funds available, and that Congress was usurping powers reserved to the states under the Tenth Amendment. In rejecting jurisdiction of this suit, the Court declared that the issue raised was political and hence not justiciable and that, in any case, no state may institute judicial proceedings to protect citizens of the United States against the operation of federal statutes.

Frothingham v. Mellon (1923). A companion suit to *Massachusetts* v. *Mellon* brought by a taxpayer for the same purpose. In rejecting it, also for want of jurisdiction, the Court held that the individual's interest as a taxpayer in the funds of the United States was so infinitesimal, and the effect of the projected grant-in-aid upon future taxation was so remote, that the individual had no basis for an appeal for injunctive relief in a court administering equity. Modified by *Flast* v. *Cohen, q.v.*

Social Security Cases (**1937**). Two cases, *Helvering* v. *Davis* (1937) and *Steward Machine Co.* v. *Davis* (1937). The Court upheld the constitutionality of taxes levied by the federal government on employers and employees in certain establishments to finance the joint federal-state system of unemployment insurance, special assistance to wage earners and others, and the federal old-age insurance program of the Social Security Act of 1935. The Court held that Congress had properly regarded social insecurity as a national problem to be attacked nationally; that the cooperative federal-state features of the social-security system did not violate the Tenth Amendment or coerce the states into abandoning their appropriate governmental functions; and that the proceeds of taxes levied to support this program were spent in aid of the general welfare.

Flast v. Cohen (**1968**). The Court held that a federal taxpayer has standing to sue to prevent the expenditure of federal funds for the establishment of religion, a field which is forbidden to Congress by the First Amendment. A taxpayer may not, however, sue to prevent an expenditure under any of the powers granted to Congress in Article I, section 8.

SCOPE OF THE COMMERCE POWER

Gibbons v. Ogden (**1824**). The Court declared that the power of Congress to regulate foreign and interstate commerce embraces every species of commercial intercourse between the United States and foreign nations and every commercial transaction that is not wholly carried on within the boundaries of a single state; that its power over interstate commerce does not stop at the boundary line of any state but is applicable within the interior of a state; and that the term "commerce" includes navigation.

Pensacola Telegraph Co. v. Western Union Telegraph Co. (**1878**). The Court held that the commerce power extends to communications. Federal powers over commerce "are not confined to the instrumentalities of commerce, or the postal service known or in use when the

Constitution was adopted, but keep pace with the progress of the country, and adapt themselves to the new developments of time and circumstances."

Pipe Line Cases (1914). The Court held that pipe lines across state boundaries, even though they were not common carriers but transported only oil and gas belonging to their owners, were instruments of interstate commerce and hence subject to the jurisdiction of Congress.

"Hot Oil" Cases (1935). *See under* Delegation of Power, page 88.

Heart of Atlanta Motel, Inc. v. United States (1964). The Court sustained, under the commerce power, an Act of Congress banning racial discrimination in public accommodations. This in effect overruled the Civil Rights cases decision. *See under* Equal Protection of the Laws, page 123.

NAVIGATION

The Daniel Ball (1871). The Court declared that navigable waters of the United States include all rivers and natural waterways which are navigable in fact and which are used, or are susceptible of being used, as highways of interstate or foreign commerce and that "whenever a commodity has begun to move from one state to another, commerce in that commodity between the states has commenced."

United States v. Appalachian Power Co. (1940). The Court held that the commerce power of the federal government extends to all rivers which are capable of being made navigable by artificial improvements, and also to the water power inherent in a flowing stream. Therefore, the Federal Power Commission may grant licenses that supersede state licenses for the construction of dams on terms considered desirable from the standpoint of national planning.

RAILROAD RATES AND SERVICES

Wabash, St. Louis, and Pacific R.R. Co. v. Illinois (1886). The Court held that the states had no constitutional power to regulate the interstate rates of railways passing through their territory even in the absence of federal legislation on the subject. The ruling nullified the effect of earlier decisions in which the contrary had been held. It thereby invalidated state laws which sought to regulate interstate rates and augmented the demand for federal regulation. Such regulation was begun in 1887 by the enactment of the Interstate Commerce Act.

Shreveport Rate Case (Houston E. & W. Texas Ry. Co. v. United States, 1914). The Texas Railway Commission was found to have fixed unreasonably low rates between distributing centers in Texas and points near the state's borders, to the disadvantage of distributors in other states whose rates were fixed by the Interstate Commerce Commission. The Court ordered the Texas Commission to raise its rates to conform with those fixed by the Interstate Commerce Commission for interstate shipments.

Wisconsin Rate Case (Wisconsin v. Chicago, B. and Q. Ry. Co., 1922). The Court extended the doctrine, first elaborated in the Shreveport Rate Case, that there is no invasion of a state's power over intrastate commerce if the Interstate Commerce Commission requires equalization of intrastate rates with interstate rates in order to overcome existing discrimination among shippers and make national control over interstate commerce effective.

STATE POLICE POWERS OVER INTERSTATE COMMERCE

Cooley v. Board of Wardens (1851). The Court developed the doctrine that the commerce power of Congress is not exclusive, but that where a uniform national rule is not required, the states may apply their own regulations to foreign and interstate commerce (as in local pilotage regulations), which remain valid until such time as Congress may decide to supersede them.

Edwards v. California (1941). The Court invalidated a California law that made it an offense to transport indigent nonresidents into the state, on the ground that the law imposed an unconstitutional burden upon interstate commerce.

South Carolina Highway Department v. Barnwell Bros. (1938). The Court held that in the absence of congressional regulation, a state may impose limits on the weight and width of motor vehicles passing interstate over its highways. The Court said that the states or their local subdivisions have built the highways and are responsible for their safety. The fact that state regulations affect interstate and intrastate commerce alike constitutes a safeguard against abuses of state regulatory power.

Southern Pacific Co. v. Arizona (1945). Invalidated an Arizona law of 1912, which prohibited operating railroad trains of more than fourteen passenger cars or seventy freight cars, because the law was found to have slight or problematical advantages as a safety measure (longer trains were safely operated elsewhere). The Court held that effects of the law had been to delay the free flow of commerce, increase its cost, and impair its efficiency.

Huron Portland Cement Co. v. City of Detroit (1960). The Court sustained the application of a municipality's smoke-abatement ordinance to ships in its port, operating in interstate commerce, whose boilers and equipment had been federally inspected and licensed. The Court held the local regulation valid because it looked to the health of the local community and imposed no discriminatory burden on interstate commerce. Federal regulation, the Court said, looks to maritime safety and has not pre-empted the field to the exclusion of local police regulation.

THE ORIGINAL PACKAGE DOCTRINE

Brown v. Maryland (1827). Reversed the conviction of Brown in a Maryland court for having imported and sold one package of dry goods without paying a heavy license fee, as required by Maryland law. The Court held that in paying federal import taxes, Brown had purchased the right to import the goods; that the Maryland license fee was a tax violating the Constitutional prohibition against state duties on imports (Article I, section 10); and that, so long as the commodity remained in the original package in which it had been imported, state taxes and police regulations could not apply to it. They began to apply only when the original package was broken and the contents were commingled with others.

Leisy v. Hardin (1890). The Court extended the original-package doctrine of *Brown* v. *Maryland* from foreign to interstate commerce. It declared that the states could not apply police regulations to prevent shipments of liquor from other states so long as the liquor remained in the packages in which it had been shipped. The rule of *Cooley* v. *Board of Wardens* (*see under* State Police Powers, page 79) did not apply since interstate shipments required national regulation. Since Congress had not issued regulations, or expressly permitted the states to make them, it was to be presumed that Congress, by its silence, intended no regulation.

Clark Distilling Co. v. Western Maryland Ry. Co. (1917). In 1913, Congress passed the Webb-Kenyon Act, which prohibited the transportation of liquor to a state where its use would violate state law. The Court upheld the act on the grounds (*a*) that Congress has the power to prevent one state from using interstate commerce to violate another state's law and (*b*) that the act had not delegated legislative power to the states since Congress had specified the conditions under which it took effect.

FEDERAL REGULATION OF BUSINESS

United States v. E. C. Knight Co. (1895). The Court held that the Sherman Antitrust Act did not apply to a combination of four Pennsylvania companies which had a virtual monopoly of the refining of sugar in the United States because (*a*) manufacture precedes commerce and is not a part of it; (*b*) interstate commerce does not commence until goods begin their final movement from one state to another; and (*c*) the monopoly of manufacture in this case had no direct relation to interstate commerce.

Northern Securities Co. v. United States (1904). The first successful prosecution under the Sherman Antitrust Act. The Court ordered the dissolution of a holding company which controlled the Great Northern and Northern Pacific railroads on the ground that it lessened competition and restrained interstate commerce.

Swift & Co. v. United States (1905). Affirmed the power of Congress to punish conspiracies in restraint of trade among buyers and sellers on the Chicago stockyards. The Court declared that in the habitual course of commerce, livestock originating in one state paused at the Chicago stockyards only long enough to find a buyer before being forwarded to another state; therefore they had remained within the "current" of commerce. The same concept was used to sustain federal regulation of livestock commission men in *Stafford* v. *Wallace* (1922) and of dealers in grain futures in *Chicago Board of Trade* v. *Olsen* (1923).

Standard Oil Co. v. United States (1911). Under the Sherman Antitrust Act, the Court ordered the dissolution of the Standard Oil Company of New Jersey not because of its huge size but because it had used its economic power through pricing and other manipulative policies to restrain trade unreasonably ("rule of reason").

Schechter Poultry Corp. v. United States (1935). The Court declared the National Industrial Recovery Act unconstitutional because it delegated legislative powers to the President and attempted, under the guise of the interstate commerce power, to regulate aspects of a business—in this instance the slaughtering and sale of poultry—which fell within the jurisdiction of the states.

National Labor Relations Board v. Jones and Laughlin Steel Corp. (1937). The Court virtually abandoned the doctrine of *United States v. E. C. Knight Co.* (see page 81) that manufacturing is not commerce. It upheld provisions of the Wagner Act forbidding unfair labor practices that affected interstate commerce. (The case concerned clerical employees who had been dismissed for union-organizing activities.) Although the defendant steel company was not directly engaged in transportation, the Court held that successful conduct of its far-flung business depended upon the free flow of interstate commerce to furnish it with raw materials and to market its products in other states and in foreign countries; hence the act prohibiting unfair labor practices was a proper exercise of constitutional power to protect and promote interstate commerce.

United States v. Interstate Commerce Commission (1970). Overruling the Northern Securities case (*q.v.*), the Court approved a renewed proposal to merge the same railroads (and others) on the ground that prospective improvement in service outweighed the benefits of competition.

FEDERAL REGULATION OF INSURANCE

Paul v. Virginia (1869). Upheld a Virginia law requiring out-of-state insurance companies to obtain a license in order to do business in the state. The Court held that issuing a policy of insurance is not a transaction in interstate commerce; such contracts are not subjects of trade and barter and are not commodities shipped across state lines to be put up for sale. It also held that the "comity clause" (Article IV, section 2) does not entitle such a corporation to enter another state; the clause applies only to natural persons and not to corporations, which are artificial creations of a state.

United States v. South-Eastern Underwriters Association (1944). The Court abandoned the precedent established in *Paul* v. *Virginia* (at a time when Congress had not regulated insurance) and held that Congress had power under the interstate commerce clause to break up a combination of companies which had monopolized insurance in several states and had engaged in coercion, intimidation, and other unfair practices against both competitors and consumers.

FEDERAL REGULATION OF AGRICULTURE

Mulford v. Smith (1939). For all practical purposes, the Court overruled its decision in *United States* v. *Butler* (*see under* The Taxing Power), and sustained the second Agricultural Adjustment Act, declaring that Congress might constitutionally regulate the flow of an agricultural commodity to the interstate market in order to foster, protect, and conserve commerce or "to prevent the flow of commerce from working harm to the people of the nation."

Wickard v. Filburn (1942). The Court held that an Ohio farmer who planted twenty-three acres of wheat for his own consumption, in excess of the quota of eleven acres set by the Secretary of Agriculture, had exerted "a substantial economic effect on interstate commerce," and so had made himself liable for penalties imposed by the Agricultural Adjustment Act of 1938. This case is noteworthy as an extreme extension of federal power over commerce.

FEDERAL LEGISLATION CONCERNING LABOR

Adair v. United States (1905). Invalidated a federal statute outlawing employment contracts in interstate commerce in which a worker agreed not to join a union (yellow-dog contract). The Court declared that the law violated the due-process clause of the Fifth Amendment by abridging freedom of contract and that there was no possible legal connection between an employee's membership in a labor union and the flow of interstate commerce.

Danbury Hatters' Case (Loewe v. Lawlor, 1908). The Court held that a nationwide boycott instituted by employees against the products of an employer was in restraint of trade under the Sherman Antitrust Act. The ruling of this decision was nullified by the Clayton Act (1914), which exempted labor unions from the operation of the Sherman Act.

Wilson v. New (1917). Upheld the constitutionality of the Adamson Act, which provided for an eight-hour day and appropriate wage standards for interstate railway employees. The Court declared that, although Congress could not control or prevent collective agreement on wages on interstate railways or fail to enforce a voluntary wage agreement, the failure of employees and employers to agree establishes a condition which Congress may resolve by fixing wages or requiring arbitration, such authority being justified by Congress's responsibility for maintaining the uninterrupted flow of commerce.

Hammer v. Dagenhart (1918). Declared unconstitutional an Act of Congress prohibiting the interstate transportation of goods made in factories employing children, on the ground that it was not a bona fide regulation of commerce among the states but an effort to control the conditions of employment and manufacture within the states. Goods made by child labor are not deleterious in themselves and are indistinguishable from those made by adults.

Bailey v. Drexel Furniture Co. (1922). *See under* The Taxing Power, page 75.

Adkins v. Children's Hospital (1923). Declared unconstitutional a minimum-wage law for the District of Columbia, which Congress had passed under its power to "exercise exclusive legislation" over the District. The Court said that the law (*a*) violated the rights of the parties freely to contract with one another; (*b*) set up standards of enforcement that were "too vague and fatally uncertain"; (*c*) required the employer to pay the minimum wage whether or not the employee was worth that much to him; and (*d*) was "so clearly the product of a naked, arbitrary exercise of power that it cannot be allowed to stand under the Constitution." Overruled by *West Coast Hotel Co.* v. *Parrish* (*see under* State Labor Legislation, page 122).

United States v. Darby (1941). The Court sustained provisions of the Fair Labor Standards Act of 1938 which fixed maximum hours and minimum wages for most employees in industry and barred from interstate commerce the shipment of goods manufactured in violation of its provisions. The Court declared that "while manufacturing is not of itself interstate commerce the shipment of manufactured goods interstate is such commerce." Overruling and repudiating the reasoning in *Hammer* v. *Dagenhart,* the Court held that the power of Congress to prevent transportation is not limited to articles which are deleterious in themselves; nor is it barred by the Tenth Amendment's reservation of powers to the states: "The amendment states but a truism that all is retained which has not been surrendered."

BORROWING AND CURRENCY

Veazie Bank v. Fenno (1869). Rejecting arguments that Congress lacked power to impair charters granted by a state (compare *McCulloch* v. *Maryland,* page 66), the Court sustained a federal tax levied on notes issued by state-chartered banks. (The legislative purpose was avowedly to drive such notes out of existence and secure a monopoly for the circulation of notes issued by the newly created national banks.) The Court held that the tax was an exercise of the constitutional power of Congress to provide a sound and uniform currency.

Hepburn v. Griswold (1870). The Court, with a membership reduced to seven, declared unconstitutional Acts of Congress that made greenbacks legal tender in payment of debts between individuals. The Court held that to require creditors to accept paper money to settle contracts made before the acts were passed would deprive them of property in violation of the due-process clause of the Fifth Amendment.

Legal Tender Cases (1871). Two cases (*Knox* v. *Lee* and *Parker* v. *Davis*). The Court, with two new Justices, appointed probably for the purpose of creating a majority, voted five to four to overturn *Hepburn* v. *Griswold*. It decided that the power of Congress to issue notes and make them legal tender for all debts was implied not only from the powers to wage war but also from the powers to borrow on the credit of the United States and to coin money. The Court said that creditors might normally expect to risk losses because of variations in the purchasing power of the medium of exchange.

Juilliard v. Greenman (1884). Upheld the use of legal tender notes in peacetime by implication from the constitutional powers to tax, borrow, coin money, and regulate the value of money.

Norman v. Baltimore & Ohio Railroad Co. (1935). The Court sustained a joint resolution of Congress to abrogate clauses in private contracts requiring payment in gold; such clauses were interpreted as requiring payment in money, not in gold bullion.

Perry v. United States (1935). The Court held that Congress had no power to abrogate the clause in United States bonds that principal and interest are payable in gold coin of the existing standard of value, because obligations under the borrowing power take precedence over the power to regulate the value of money. The Court stated, however, that holders of United States bonds could not recover the principal and interest in gold unless they could show actual loss of buying power. Congress later closed the door to suits for recovery.

WAR POWERS*

Selective Draft Law Cases (1918). Cases arising from the refusal of persons to register for compulsory military service under the Selective Service Act of 1917. The Court supported the compulsory features of the act, holding (*a*) that the power of Congress to raise and support armies is separate and distinct from its power to call the states' militia into federal service; (*b*) that the constitutional power to raise armies includes the power to compel military service; and (*c*) that compulsory service is an obligation of a citizen to his government, sanctioned by numerous precedents in American history. Subsequent cases emphasized and extended this decision.

Block v. Hirsh (1921). The Court upheld state and federal emergency rent laws enacted at the close of World War I. The legislation, which fixed rents and temporarily extended leases, was held to be consistent with due process on the theory that the wartime emergency had clothed the relationship of landlord and tenant with a preponderant public interest and, at least temporarily, had made that relationship subject to the same sort of regulatory power that government was accustomed to exert over the rates and services of public utilities.

Ashwander v. Tennessee Valley Authority (1936). The case concerned a contract for the sale to a private company of surplus electric power generated at the Wilson Dam. The Court upheld the peacetime maintenance of the dam and the hydroelectric installations constructed in World War I, both under the commerce power to improve navigation and under the war power to provide for the future supply of munitions. It upheld the acquisition by the Tennessee Valley Authority of transmission lines for the distribution and sale of its electric power on the principle that, if the government owns property, Congress, acting in the public interest, may determine the manner and conditions of its disposition.

Yakus v. United States (1944). *See under* Delegation of Power, page 88.

Toth v. Quarles (1955). *See under* The President as Commander in Chief, page 96.

Woods v. Miller (1948). Sustained the Housing and Rent Control Act of 1947. The Court held that Congress, even after the cessation

* *See also* The President as Commander in Chief, page 95.

of hostilities, may remedy conditions resulting from wartime mobilization of men and materials, under its war powers and the "necessary and proper" clause of Article I, section 8.

GOVERNMENT OF TERRITORIES AND DEPENDENCIES

American Insurance Co. v. Canter (1828). The Court held that although the power to acquire territory is nowhere granted in specific terms, Congress possesses that right through its power to make war, which may result in conquest of territory, and its treaty-making power. The Court also stated that in establishing courts for a territory, Congress is not bound by the provisions of Article III, but may provide for the appointment of judges with four-year terms, under its power to make needful rules for the territories.

Cherokee Cases (1831, 1832). Georgia sought to gain jurisdiction over lands held by the Cherokee Indians under treaties with the United States. In *Cherokee Nation* v. *Georgia* (1831), the Court held that it had no jurisdiction to hear a case brought against a state by an Indian tribe because it was a "domestic dependent nation." It added, *obiter dicta,* that the Cherokees had an unquestionable right to the lands until they voluntarily ceded them to the United States. In *Worcester* v. *Georgia* (1832) the court ruled that the Cherokee nation was a distinct political community within which "the laws of Georgia can have no force, and which the citizens of Georgia have no right to enter but with the assent of the Cherokees themselves or in conformity with treaties and with the acts of Congress." Georgia refused to obey the decision and President Jackson refused to enforce it. In 1835, most of the Cherokees were moved west to lands now in Oklahoma, which the federal government set aside for them.

Insular Cases (1901, 1903). A group of cases concerning the status of territories acquired after the Spanish-American War. In *DeLima* v. *Bidwell,* the Court held that regular duties on Puerto Rican goods could not be collected in New York because Puerto Rico is not a foreign country. In *Downes* v. *Bidwell,* the Court held that special duties imposed by Congress on Puerto Rican and Philippine products could be collected because these territories, though not foreign, had never been incorporated into the United States by treaty of cession, as had the older territories on the North American continent; hence the requirement of uniformity of taxation in Article I, section 9, did not apply. In *Hawaii* v. *Mankichi* (1903), the Court held that indictment by a grand jury and conviction only after a unanimous verdict of a trial jury were not required in the judicial proceedings of unincorporated territories; their inhabitants were entitled to all the fundamental rights guaranteed by the Constitution, but not to those that were "procedural, remedial, or formal."

DELEGATION OF POWER

Field v. Clark (1892). Involved presidential authority under the Tariff Act of 1890 to suspend that act's free list in the case of countries that imposed duties upon American products which were "reciprocally unequal and unreasonable." The act had been attacked as an unconstitutional delegation of law-making power. The Court affirmed the principle that legislative power cannot be delegated but asserted that no such delegation had occurred in this case since the contingency when the discretionary power of the President was to take effect had been "named" and nothing involving the "expediency or just operation" of the statute had been confided to the President.

"Hot Oil" Cases (1935). Three cases, the principal one being *Panama Refining Co.* v. *Ryan,* in which the Court held that Congress had unconstitutionally delegated legislative powers to the President by authorizing him in 1933 to prohibit the shipment in interstate and foreign commerce of oil in excess of the amount permitted to be produced or withdrawn from storage under the laws of any state.

United States v. Curtiss-Wright Export Corp. (1936). The Court upheld a statute authorizing the President to exercise broad discretion, with no criterion specified for its use, in issuing a proclamation to embargo a shipment of arms to foreign belligerents. Because of the plenary nature of the federal government's authority over international relations, the Court said Congress might exercise greater latitude in delegating power to the President over foreign affairs than in delegating discretion to him over internal matters. (*See also under* The President and Foreign Affairs, page 93.)

Yakus v. United States (1944). Sustained the discretionary power of a federal administrator to enforce the Emergency Price Control Act of 1942. The Court declared that such authority was comparable to that given an administrative agency to fix fair and reasonable rates for a public utility and did not constitute a delegation of legislative power.

BILL OF ATTAINDER

Cummings v. Missouri (1867). Declared unconstitutional, under Article I, section 10, a state law which required members of certain professions to take a special oath that they had never by act or word manifested sympathy with those engaged in rebellion. The Court held that the law was a bill of attainder, defined as a legislative act which applies to "named individuals or to easily ascertainable members of a group in such a way as to inflict punishment on them without judicial trial." Since the acts punishable had not previously been crimes, the Court said that the state act was also an *ex post facto* law (prohibited by Article I, section 9).

United States v. Lovett (1946). Held unconstitutional, as a bill of attainder, a statute (a rider to an appropriation act) which forbade payment of salaries to federal employees, mentioned by name in the act, whose conduct and political associations had been termed "subversive" by the House Committee on Un-American Activities.

United States v. Brown (1965). Held that a provision of the Labor Management Reporting and Disclosure Act of 1959, making it a crime for a Communist Party member to serve as an officer or employee of a labor union, was unconstitutional as a bill of attainder. Though Congress may legislate to prevent political strikes primarily designed to disrupt commerce and industry, it may not by legislation punish persons who belong to a party which might foment political strikes.

OBLIGATION OF A CONTRACT

Fletcher v. Peck (1810). *See under* Judicial Review, page 65.

Dartmouth College v. Woodward (1819). The Court decided that an act of the New Hampshire legislature altering the charter of Dartmouth College without its consent was in violation of the Constitution (Article I, section 10), which forbids a state to impair the obligation of a contract, a decision afterward applied in favor of nonacademic (business) interests. Later the Court ruled that corporation charters must be strictly construed, and were subordinate to the public interest. (*See Charles River Bridge* v. *Warren Bridge,* page 90.)

Ogden v. Saunders (1827). The Court held that in the absence of federal bankruptcy legislation, the release of insolvent debtors from their debts under a state bankruptcy law did not impair the obligation of a contract entered into after the state law was passed. An existing law on the subject is, in effect, a part of the contract, and a state law is presumed constitutional until the violation of the Constitution is proved "beyond all reasonable doubt." (This decision is the basis for sustaining later state legislation reserving rights to the state to modify corporation charters.)

Charles River Bridge v. Warren Bridge (1837). Sustained the creation by the Massachusetts legislature of a competing company to build a bridge not far from an existing private toll bridge. The Court modified substantially the rule in the Dartmouth College case by holding that the public interest and common-law rules of construction require that franchises granted to private corporations be construed strictly and that they afford their holders no implied protection against legislative action which might injure the value of the franchise. This rule of strict construction applies to all corporate franchises.

Fertilizing Company v. Hyde Park (1878). *See under* Due Process under The Fourteenth Amendment, page 120.

Home Building and Loan Association v. Blaisdell (1934). Upheld a state statute deferring a mortgagor's right to redeem foreclosed property two years beyond the time stipulated when the mortgage was made. The Court held that the contract clause in Article I, section 10, was not breached, since existing contracts are subject to regulation in the public interest under the state's police power. Just as a state may come to the relief of its citizens in case of natural disasters, so may it act in an economic crisis to safeguard the economic structure on which the good of all depends.

THE PRESIDENCY

Kendall v. United States (1838). The Court held that an officer, in this case the Postmaster General, may not refuse to perform a duty imposed upon him by an Act of Congress, even though the President has ordered him not to perform it. In addition to political tasks carried out under the direction of the President, Congress may assign to any executive officer any duty it may think proper which is not repugnant to rights protected by the Constitution. "To contend that the obligation imposed on the President to see the laws faithfully executed implies a power to forbid their execution, is a novel construction of the Constitution and is entirely inadmissible."

Mississippi v. Johnson (1867). A decision arising from the attempt of Mississippi to obtain an injunction to prevent the President from enforcing one of the Reconstruction Acts on the ground that the law was unconstitutional. The Court held that the responsibility of the President to enforce the laws is not a mere ministerial duty, in which nothing is left to discretion, but rather an executive and political duty. Therefore, an injunction may not be issued against the President to restrain him from enforcing a law.

In re Neagle (1890). The Attorney General assigned a United States deputy marshal (Neagle) as a bodyguard to Justice Field, whose life had been threatened. While Justice Field was on circuit duty in California, the marshal killed an assailant to prevent him from killing the Justice. A California court indicted Neagle for murder. Under federal law he could be released by writ of habeas corpus from state authority *only* if he had been acting under a law of the United States. No Act of Congress had authorized the Attorney General to assign a bodyguard to a Justice. However, the Court held that a writ of habeas corpus was issuable on the basis of an executive order, because the President's duty to execute the law includes the implied power to protect government officials who are on duty.

In re Debs (1895). Upheld a federal injunction against striking Pullman Company employees who had halted railroad transportation in the Chicago area; and sustained President Cleveland in sending troops to the area when the injunction was disobeyed. The President's action was not in compliance with the request of the Governor, Altgeld of Illinois (*see* Article IV, section 4); in fact, the Governor strongly protested the order. The Court asserted that "the strong arm of the national Government may be put forth to brush away all obstructions to the freedom of interstate commerce or the transportation of the mails."

Youngstown Sheet & Tube Co. v. Sawyer (1952). The Court refused to uphold President Truman's seizure of steel mills in order to avert a strike which he said might dangerously reduce the supply of munitions for the Korean War. The Court held (six to three with seven separate opinions presented) that in passing the Taft-Hartley Act, Congress had considered granting the power to seize strikebound plants to the President but decided against it. The Court could not find such presidential authority in the clauses of Article II of the Constitution, vesting the executive power in the President, making him Commander in Chief, and imposing on him the duty to enforce the laws.

THE REMOVAL POWER

Myers v. United States (1926). Declared unconstitutional the Tenure of Office Act of 1876 which required the consent of the Senate to the removal of certain classes of postmasters. The Court held that the President may remove at pleasure any officer appointed by himself and the Senate under the executive power vested in him by Article II. He is responsible for the execution of the laws, and he can execute the laws only through subordinates. He must, therefore, have the power to remove subordinates who have shown lack of ability or disloyalty to the administration.

Humphrey's Executor (Rathbun) v. United States (1935). The Court modified the ruling in *Myers* v. *United States* by denying to the President the power to remove quasi-legislative and quasi-judicial officers when Congress had made other provisions for their removal. The Court declared that Congress when it created the Federal Trade Commission had acted constitutionally in specifying that the President could remove a commissioner only for inefficiency, neglect of duty, or malfeasance in office, because the duties of such officers are not political or executive but are independent of the President's control. "It is quite evident that one who holds his office only during the pleasure of another cannot be depended upon to maintain an attitude of independence against the latter's will."

Wiener v. United States (1958). The Court held that even though Congress had not limited the President's power to remove members of the War Claims Commission, their functions were intrinsically judicial; hence the President could not remove them except for cause.

THE PRESIDENT AND FOREIGN AFFAIRS

Foster v. Neilson (1829). The Court refused to review the merits of a dispute over land grants in territory east of the Mississippi River claimed by both the United States and Spain. The Spanish grant had been made in 1804. Later the United States government had claimed the territory as part of the Louisiana Purchase and occupied it by force. The Court declared that the decisions of the President and Congress are binding on the judiciary in all matters affecting the rights of the United States in foreign affairs.

United States v. Curtiss-Wright Export Corporation (1936). Upheld an arms embargo imposed by the President under authority given to him by joint resolution of Congress. "The President is the sole organ of the Federal government in the field of international relations—a power which does not require as a basis for its exercise an act of Congress, but which, of course like every other governmental power, must be exercised in subordination to the applicable provisions of the Constitution." (*See also under* Delegation of Power, page 88.)

Kent v. Dulles (1958). The Court held that the Secretary of State, in issuing passports under "such rules as the President shall designate," is limited by restrictions to those specifically authorized by Congress or established by usage. "The right to travel is part of the 'liberty' of which the citizen cannot be deprived without the due process of law of the Fifth Amendment."

Aptheker v. Secretary of State (1964). Declared unconstitutional the provisions of the Internal Security Act of 1950 which denied passports to persons belonging to organizations required by the Act to register with the Attorney General. The Court refused to uphold the restrictions on the grounds (*a*) that they were too broad; (*b*) that they did not consider whether a person's membership in such an organization was knowing or unknowing or whether his participation was active or inactive; and (*c*) that they did not consider the purpose for which he wished to travel.

TREATIES AND EXECUTIVE AGREEMENTS

Head Money Cases (1884). Sustained an Act of Congress which levied a tax on steamship companies amounting to a small sum per capita on every immigrant brought to the United States, though some of these immigrants came from countries with which the United States had treaties guaranteeing their free admission. The Court held that treaties and statutes are on an equal plane. Hence if a self-executory treaty (one which requires no statute for its enforcement) and an Act of Congress are in conflict, the later treaty or statute prevails.

Fong Yue Ting v. United States (1893). The Court declined to interfere with a deportation order against a native of China who had come to the United States before 1879, when a treaty with China allowed free admission of its citizens, who had remained an alien, and who had failed to register as required by an 1892 Act of Congress. The Court declared that the right to exclude or to expel aliens is an inherent and inalienable right of every sovereign and independent state and that the Constitution has vested in the President and Congress plenary powers to secure this right, to be exercised by means of treaties and statutes.

Missouri v. Holland (1920). Sustained a federal statute to enforce a treaty with Great Britain for the mutual protection of migratory birds flying between the United States and British possessions to the north and south. The Court said that migratory birds are "a national interest of very nearly the first magnitude," which can be protected only by national action in concert with another country; and that birds which are only briefly in a state can not be claimed as its property. (A federal statute for the protection of migratory birds, antedating the treaty, had been invalidated by lower federal courts as usurpation of the reserved powers of the states and an encroachment on their property rights.)

United States v. Belmont (1937). Sustained an executive agreement which President Franklin D. Roosevelt, without consulting the Senate, entered into when he recognized the Soviet Union in 1933. The Court held that the recognition, the establishing of diplomatic relations, and the agreement assigning American assets of a former Russian corporation were all part of one transaction, which was a "treaty" within the meaning of the Court of Appeals Act, and that the Executive spoke as the "sole organ" of the Government in the transaction. To the objection that the Soviet Union had acquired the assets by confiscation, which was against the law of New York State, the Court replied that by recognition, the United States had accepted all the acts of the Soviet Union with respect to its own citizens, and that the agreement overrode conflicting state laws.

Reid v. Covert (1957). The Court held that an international agreement whereby American servicemen and their dependents who committed crimes on British soil were to be tried by American courts did not authorize the United States to try the wife of a soldier by a military court. She was not a member of "the land and naval forces," for whose regulation Congress may provide in Article I, section 8; she was rather a civilian, under the Fifth and Sixth Amendments, answerable to indictment only by a grand jury and entitled to trial by jury.

THE PRESIDENT AS COMMANDER IN CHIEF

Martin v. Mott (1827). The Court held that when acting by authority of a 1795 Act of Congress (under Article I, section 8), the President is the sole judge of when an exigency has arisen which necessitates calling forth the militia, and his judgment in such a situation is conclusive on all other persons.

The Prize Cases (1863). Four cases concerning vessels captured while running a naval blockade which President Lincoln had imposed by proclamation on Southern ports shortly after the firing on Fort Sumter in 1861. The Court sustained the President's action, saying: "If a war be made by invasion of a foreign nation, the President is not only authorized but bound to resist force, by force. He does not initiate the war, but is bound to accept the challenge without waiting for any special legislative authority. And whether the hostile party be a foreign invader, or States organized in rebellion, it is none the less a war. . . ." Congress later passed legislation ratifying the presidential proclamation.

Ex Parte Milligan (1866). The case of a civilian who was convicted, by a military commission sitting at Indianapolis in 1864, of fomenting insurrection and other treasonable activities and who applied to the United States Circuit Court for a writ of habeas corpus. On appeal the Court held that Milligan had been unlawfully convicted, because President Lincoln had acted unconstitutionally in setting up the military commission in a place where the civil courts were open and their processes were unobstructed: such action was permissible only in an actual theater of war where civil courts were not functioning.

Ex Parte Quirin (1942). The case of seven Germans who were landed secretly on American shores in World War II for the purpose of committing sabotage and who after capture were tried and sentenced by a military commission. The Court determined that the military commission had been properly constituted; that the spies though in a district where courts were open (*cf. Ex Parte Milligan*) were subject to the jurisdiction of the military as "unlawful belligerents" under the laws of war; and that the guarantee of a jury trial under the Sixth Amendment did not apply since that guarantee applies to civil, and not to military courts.

Korematsu v. United States (1944). Korematsu, an American citizen of Japanese ancestry, was among those removed from their homes in states near the West Coast to relocation centers in the interior in accordance with military determination under an executive order of 1942. (Congress later made it a crime to violate this order.) The Court sustained Korematsu's removal because (*a*) "the properly constituted military authorities" feared an invasion of the West Coast and decided that the military urgency required the removal of persons of Japanese origin from the area; (*b*) there was insufficient time to segregate the loyal from the disloyal Japanese; and (*c*) "Congress, reposing its confidence in this time of war in our military leaders—as inevitably it must—determined that they should have the power to do just this."

Toth v. Quarles (1955). The Court held unconstitutional an Act of Congress requiring that discharged servicemen be tried by a court martial for crimes allegedly committed during their service. The Court said that such a requirement would lessen for the serviceman the safeguards enjoyed by other civilians under Article III of the Constitution and would encroach upon the jurisdiction of regular courts.

THE PARDONING POWER

Ex Parte Garland (1867). The Court declared unconstitutional, as a bill of attainder, an Act of Congress which required lawyers practicing before federal courts to take an oath that they had never voluntarily borne arms against the United States or given aid to its enemies. (Garland, although he had been pardoned by President Johnson, could not take the oath.) The Court held that (under Article II, section 2) a full pardon "releases the punishment and blots out of existence the guilt so that in the eye of the law the offender is as innocent as if he had never committed the offense"; and that the pardoning power extends to every offense against the law and may be exercised before legal proceedings are begun, or while they are pending, or after conviction and judgment.

Ex Parte Grossman (1925). Ruled that the President may pardon and remit a sentence imposed by a federal court for criminal contempt on the ground that there are numerous precedents for such pardons in England and the United States, and indeed they are especially useful when sentences are imposed "without the restraining influence of a jury and without many of the guarantees which the Bill of Rights offers to protect the individual against unjust conviction." But a pardon "can only be granted for a contempt fully completed." It cannot stop "coercive measures" to enforce rights of a complainant.

JUDICIAL ORGANIZATION

American Insurance Co. v. Canter (1828). *See under* Government of Territories and Dependencies, page 87.

Evans v. Gore (1920). Held that the doctrine of separation of powers and the clause in Article III, section 1, which guarantees a federal judge's salary against diminution during his tenure prevent the levying on a judge's salary of an income tax enacted after the judge assumed office.

Ex Parte Bakelite Corporation (1929). Differentiated the constitutional courts created under Article III from the so-called legislative courts with specialized jurisdictions to adjudicate claims, settle disputes over customs duties and patents, and administer justice in the territories which had been created by Congress under Article I and Article IV. The Court held that, in creating the latter type of courts, Congress is not bound by the limitations of Article III concerning jurisdiction or the tenure and compensation of judges.

Glidden Co. v. Zdanok (1962). After an Act of Congress had provided that the Court of Claims and the Court of Customs and Patent Appeals should become constitutional courts under Article III, the Court ruled that judges of these specialized courts could not be assigned to sit on district or circuit courts, the regular courts of the federal judicial system.

JURISDICTION OF THE FEDERAL COURTS

Chisholm v. Georgia (1793). The Court construed the provision of Article III, section 2, granting it jurisdiction over controversies "between a state and citizens of another state," as including the power to hear and decide a case brought by Chisholm, a citizen of South Carolina, against the state of Georgia to obtain compensation for property taken during the Revolution. The decision alarmed the states that had debts outstanding and led directly to the adoption of the Eleventh Amendment.

Marbury v. Madison (1803). *See under* Judicial Review, page 65.

Martin v. Hunter's Lessee (1816). The Court reaffirmed its previous decision "in this very cause" which the highest Virginia state court had refused to obey. The Virginia Court alleged that the appellate jurisdiction of the United States Supreme Court did not extend over a state court and that a provision of the Judiciary Act of 1789 so extending it was unconstitutional. The Supreme Court declared: (*a*) that the Constitution "was ordained and established, not by the States in their sovereign capacities, but emphatically, as the preamble of the Constitution declares, by 'the people of the United States' "; (*b*) that the Constitution "is crowded with provisions which restrain or annul the sovereignty of the States in some of the highest branches of their prerogatives" (Article I, section 10); (*c*) that exercise of federal judicial power over the judgments of state courts is not more dangerous than over state legislatures and executives; and (*d*) that, in order to avoid differences among state courts in the interpretation of the Constitution and federal laws and treaties, it is necessary that there should be a reviewing authority to control and harmonize the "jarring and discordant judgments" which might be handed down by "judges of equal learning and integrity" in the different states. The Court's order was directed to the lower court in Virginia where the case originated.

Cohens v. Virginia (1821). The Court held that, though state courts may exercise final authority in cases which fall entirely within their jurisdiction, they are subject to the appellate jurisdiction of federal courts if their judgments involve the construction of federal laws, treaties, or the Constitution. The Court also declared that review by a federal court of a judgment secured by a state against a defendant in its own courts does not constitute a suit against a state such as is prohibited by the Eleventh Amendment.

Nashville, Chattanooga and St. Louis Railway v. Wallace (1933). The Court accepted jurisdiction to hear an appeal from a state court's declaratory judgment, which was then a recent innovation. The Court said that the Constitution did not "crystallize into changeless form" the procedure of 1789, and "so long as the case retains the essentials of an adversary proceeding, involving a real, not a hypothetical controversy, which is finally determined by the judgment below," it is a "controversy" as the word is used in conferring jurisdiction in Article III.

Ex Parte McCardle (1869). Held that the power of Congress to make exceptions to the Court's appellate jurisdiction could be exercised even after the hearings on a case had been concluded. McCardle was tried for sedition by a military commission established in Mississippi by one of the Reconstruction Acts of Congress. He appealed to the Supreme Court. Some members of Congress apparently felt that the Court would follow its precedent in *Ex Parte Milligan* (*see under* The President as Commander in Chief, page 95) and interfere with Congress's program of Reconstruction. Congress repealed the Act giving the Court jurisdiction to hear McCardle's case on appeal. The Court held: "Without jurisdiction the court cannot proceed at all in any cause. Jurisdiction is power to declare the law, and when it ceases to exist, the only function remaining to the court is that of announcing the fact and dismissing the cause."

INTERSTATE CONTROVERSIES

Kentucky v. Dennison (1861). Kentucky sought a writ of mandamus to compel William Dennison, the Governor of Ohio, to extradite William Lago, a free Negro who had helped a slave to escape from Kentucky and had then fled to Ohio. The Court stated that, although it was the duty of the governor to return the fugitive, the federal government could not constitutionally compel him to perform it.

Kansas v. Colorado (1907). Kansas sued to prevent Colorado from diverting an excessive amount of water from the Colorado River for irrigation purposes. When the jurisdiction of the Court was questioned on the ground that this was not a "controversy" within the meaning of Article III, the Court asserted that, in the absence of specific limitations, the federal courts are vested with all the judicial power which the United States as a nation is capable of exercising. The Court rejected the federal government's claim to exclusive authority over irrigation as in violation of the state's right to land and water surface under the Tenth Amendment.

Virginia v. West Virginia (1918). A long-drawn-out series of cases, beginning in 1907, in which the Court determined what was an equitable division of the pre-Civil War debt of Virginia. When the state was divided and West Virginia was admitted to the Union, she agreed to assume her just share of Virginia's public debt. Later she declined to pay anything on the ground that the borrowed money had been spent in the eastern part of the state. The Court held that the debt should be divided on the basis of taxable property in the two sections as of the date of West Virginia's admission to the

Union. When West Virginia still delayed payment, the Court asserted, as "elementary," that judicial power involves the right to enforce its decisions, and suggested that Congress might act to compel payment or that an order might be issued against West Virginia. Before the Court took further action West Virginia issued bonds to pay the debt.

DIVERSITY OF CITIZENSHIP

Swift v. Tyson (1842). The Court held that in trying cases involving commercial transactions between citizens of different states, lower federal courts must apply relevant state statutes, but were not bound to follow common law decisions of state courts. Where no state statute law existed, federal courts were free to follow general principles of commercial law. State courts continued to follow their own precedents, and the result was the development of conflicting state and federal laws. Overruled by *Erie Railroad* v. *Tompkins.*

Erie Railroad v. Tompkins (1938). Reversed a lower federal court which had followed *Swift* v. *Tyson*. Tompkins, a citizen of Pennsylvania, was injured while walking along the right of way of the Erie Railroad Company, a New York corporation. Under the law of Pennsylvania, where the accident occurred, Tompkins was a trespasser and was not entitled to damages. The lower federal court decided that the railroad was negligent and was liable to pay damages. The Supreme Court held that the doctrine in *Swift* v. *Tyson* was mischievous because: (*a*) it allowed one party to select the court where the law was most favorable to him; (*b*) it rendered impossible the equal protection of the law; and (*c*) it was "an unconstitutional assumption of powers by courts of the United States which no lapse of time or respectable array of opinion should make us hesitate to correct." In matters not governed by the Constitution or Acts of Congress, "the law to be applied in any case is the law of the State. And whether the law of the State shall be declared by its legislature in a statute or by its highest court in a decision is not a matter of federal concern. There is no federal general common law."

THE BILL OF RIGHTS

Barron v. Baltimore (1833). Barron claimed that Baltimore's refusal to compensate him for a wharf rendered unusable by a city street-grading project was a violation of the Fifth Amendment. The Court held that the Bill of Rights applies only to acts of the federal government and not to those of the states or their subdivisions. The Court reasoned (*a*) that the Constitution of the United States was a document of granted powers, and therefore the Bill of Rights could limit only what was granted; and (*b*) that the Bill of Rights had been added to the Constitution because the people feared that the *federal* government might oppress them.

Gitlow v. New York (1925). Upheld a state statute which made it a crime for anyone to advocate the duty, necessity, or propriety of overthrowing organized government by force and violence, on the ground that: "the legislative body itself has previously determined the danger of substantive evil arising from utterances of a specified character." In the middle of the opinion, almost as an aside, was the statement: "For present purposes we may and do assume that freedom of speech and of the press—which are protected by the First Amendment from abridgment by Congress—are among the fundamental personal rights and 'liberties' protected by the due process clause of the Fourteenth Amendment from impairment by the states." The Court offered no logical or historical justification for abandoning the rule of *Barron* v. *Baltimore*. From this beginning almost all of the first eight Amendments have by degrees been brought under the broad shelter of the Fourteenth Amendment.

FREEDOM OF SPEECH

Schenck v. United States (1919). Sustained the conviction of a Socialist Party official who had violated the Espionage Act of 1917 by urging young men who had been called for military service to assert their constitutional rights by opposing the draft. Justice Holmes, who wrote the opinion, suggested limitations for government encroachment on the First Amendment's guarantee of freedom of speech: "The question in every case is whether the words used are used in such circumstances and are of such a nature as to create a clear and present danger that they will bring about the substantive evils that Congress has a right to prevent. . . . When a nation is at war many things that might be said in time of peace are such a hindrance to its effort that their utterance will not be endured."

Whitney v. California (1927). Sustained the conviction, under the California Criminal Syndicalism Act of 1919, of Anita Whitney, an organizer and executive committee member of the Communist Labor Party of California, which advocated sabotage, violence, and terror as means of effecting economic and political change. Though Miss Whitney testified that she did not believe in violence, the Court held that united and joint action by such a group involves greater danger to the public peace and security than the isolated utterances of individuals.

Chaplinsky v. New Hampshire (1942). The Court held that the right of free speech does not include use of lewd, obscene, profane, and libelous expressions or words such as "damned racketeer" or "God-damned Fascist" which by their very utterance inflict injury or tend to incite an immediate breach of the peace. They are "no essential part of any exposition of ideas" and are of such slight social value that they are not protected by the First Amendment.

American Communications Association v. Douds (1950). Upheld a provision of the Taft-Hartley Labor Management Relations Act of 1947 which denied access to the facilities of the National Labor Relations Board to unions whose officials refused to take non-Communist loyalty oaths. The Court held that it was not a violation of the First Amendment for Congress to legislate under its commerce power to prevent political strikes fomented by agitators who had infiltrated into labor unions.

Dennis v. United States (1951). Upheld the conviction of eleven leaders of the American Communist Party under the Smith Act's prohibition of willfully advocating and teaching overthrow of the government of the United States by force and violence. Citing Judge Learned Hand's interpretation of Justice Holmes's "clear-and-present-danger rule, whether the "gravity of the 'evil,' discounted by its improbability, justifies such invasion of free speech as is necessary to avoid the danger," the Court decided that the danger here justified restraining freedom of speech. The Government cannot wait "until the putsch is about to be executed, the plans have been laid and the signal is awaited."

Adler v. Board of Education (1952). Sustained New York State's 1949 Feinberg law, which prohibited from teaching or holding any other position in the public schools any person who advocated the overthrow of the government by force or violence. The law authorized the Board of Regents to establish a list of organizations that advocated such action, and membership in an organization on that list constituted evidence to disqualify a person from holding a position in the public schools. The Court held that "school authorities have the right and duty to screen the officials, teachers, and employees as to their fitness in order to maintain the integrity of the schools."

Yates v. United States (1957). The Court held that mere advocacy of a revolutionary philosophy, such as that of Karl Marx, was not enough to convict a Communist Party member under the Smith Act. In order to convict, the prosecution must prove the individual guilty or advocating forcible overthrow of the government and of inciting others to specific action toward this end.

Barenblatt v. United States (1959). *See under* Investigative Powers of Congress, page 74.

Scales v. United States (1961). The Court, in reviewing provisions of the Smith Act, held, five to four, that the First Amendment did not protect the speech or the right of association of an active member of a group (though ostensibly a political party) if the group advocated violent overthrow of the government. Nor did the due-process clause of the Fifth Amendment protect an individual who was an active and knowing member of an organization that was conspiring to overthrow the government by force, even though the threat was not immediate.

Communist Party of America v. Subversive Activities Control Board (1961). This case arose out of the effort to compel the American Communist Party to register under the terms of the Internal Security Act of 1950. The Court accepted the congressional conclusion that Communism is a movement dominated by a particular foreign country which is dangerous to the United States and its free institutions. Hence, it concluded that requiring the Communist Party in the United States to register with the Justice Department, list its members, and file financial statements, did not violate the freedom of expression and association protected by the First Amendment.

Keyishian v. Board of Regents (1967). Overruled *Adler* v. *Board of Education* (see page 102) and invalidated New York State's requirement of a teacher's loyalty oath. The Court held that a state may protect its educational system against subversion, but not by vague and uncertain methods that do not inform teachers of the sanctions involved in a complicated scheme of control and that "cast a pall of orthodoxy over the classroom." The Court further stated that membership in the Communist Party is not sufficient to disqualify a teacher from the public school system unless specific intent is shown to further the unlawful aims of the Party.

Brandenburg v. Ohio (1969). Overruled *Whitney* v. *California* (*see* page 101) and held that the First Amendment does not permit a state to forbid advocacy of force, violence, and terror as means to effect change, except where such advocacy is directed to inciting or producing imminent lawless action and is likely to produce such action.

SYMBOLIC SPEECH

Stromberg v. California (1931). Invalidated California's "anti-red-flag" law in a case resulting from the display of a red flag at a children's camp. The Court held that the peaceful display of a red flag as a "sign, symbol or emblem of opposition to organized government" is protected by the First Amendment's guarantee of free speech. In Chief Justice Hughes's words: "The maintenance of the opportunity for free political discussion to the end that government may be responsive to the will of the people and that changes may be obtained by lawful means . . . is a fundamental principle of our constitutional system."

Thornhill v. Alabama (1940). Declared unconstitutional a state law against "loitering or picketing," which, as interpreted by the state courts, prohibited a single picket from carrying a placard on the street in front of a factory. The Court, through Justice Murphy, declared that the safeguarding of peaceful picketing is essential to enlightening the public concerning the nature and causes of a labor dispute and thereby to securing an informed public opinion with respect to a matter of public concern.

United States v. O'Brien (1968). Sustained the conviction of a young man who violated a federal law by burning his draft card, explaining that he did so in order to influence others to adopt his antiwar beliefs. The Court said that an incidental limitation on First Amendment freedoms is justified if (*a*) it is within the constitutional power of the government; (*b*) it furthers an important or substantial government interest; (*c*) the governmental interest is unrelated to the suppression of free expression; and (*d*) the incidental restriction on alleged First Amendment freedoms is no greater than is essential to the furtherance of that interest.

FREEDOM OF SPEECH AND ASSEMBLY

De Jonge v. Oregon (1937). Brought the First Amendment guarantee of peaceable assembly under the protection of the Fourteenth Amendment. The Court reversed a state court's conviction of a speaker at a meeting called by the Communist Party to protest police methods of handling a strike. The Court held that the right of peaceable assembly is essential in order "to maintain the opportunity for free political discussion to the end that Government may be responsive to the will of the people, and that changes, if desired, may be obtained by peaceful means."

Hague v. C.I.O. (**1939**). Invalidated a Jersey City ordinance which required a permit from the director of public safety for a public assembly in the streets. The Court held that people have a right to assemble in the streets to communicate their views to others and to discuss public questions in an orderly and peaceful manner.

Edwards v. South Carolina (1963). The Court held that "South Carolina infringed the petitioners' constitutionally protected rights of free speech, free assembly, and freedom to petition for redress of their grievances" when it broke up an orderly demonstration by two hundred students on the state capitol grounds and arrested their leaders.

Cox v. Louisiana (1965). Reversed a state court's conviction of a civil rights demonstrator for blocking a street. The Court held that since it had permitted labor unions and other organizations to block streets in Louisiana, the state had not drawn fair rules as to what was illegal. The Court, however, warned that it would not sanction "demonstrations, however peaceful or commendable their motives, which conflict with properly drawn statutes and ordinances designed to promote law and order, protect the community against disorder, regulate traffic, safeguard legitimate interests in private and public property, or protect the administration of justice and other essential Governmental functions."

FREEDOM OF THE PRESS

Near v. Minnesota (1931). Declared unconstitutional a state law, ostensibly for the public good but in fact directed at a weekly newspaper in Minneapolis which was accustomed to making violent attacks on the integrity of law enforcement officials. The law prohibited the publication of scandalous, malicious, defamatory, or obscene matter and provided for enforcement by injunction against persons committing such an offense. The Court held that the object of the law was to prevent future publication and thus to place the publishers under "an effective censorship," whereas liberty of the press means "principally, although not exclusively, immunity from previous restraint or censorship."

Grosjean v. American Press Co. (1936). Invalidated a Louisiana statute which imposed a heavy and discriminatory tax on the advertising revenues of newspapers in the larger cities of the state, most of which newspapers had opposed the Huey Long machine. The Court held that this action was "a deliberate and calculated device in the guise of a tax to limit the circulation of information to which the public in entitled."

New York Times Co. v. Sullivan (1964). The Court held that libel laws cannot be used to "cast a pall of fear and timidity" on the press. Alabama courts had awarded heavy damages to Birmingham law enforcement officers who had sued the *New York Times* for libeling them in a paid political advertisement which it published. The Court reversed this decision, holding that "debate on public issues should be uninhibited, robust and wide open"; that injury to an official's reputation "affords no warrant for suppressing speech that would otherwise be free"; and that a public official may not recover damages for libel unless he can prove actual malice, that is, that the statement was made "with knowledge that it was false or with reckless disregard of whether it was false or not."

Branzburg v. Hayes (1972). The Court rejected arguments that ability to preserve the secrecy of news sources is essential to a free press and held, five to four, that a reporter must testify, and reveal the contents of his notebooks, before a grand jury.

OBSCENITY

Roth v. United States (1957). Overturned a decision that found a publication obscene, and hence not mailable, because it tended to cause immoral thoughts in minds open to such influences. The Court here cited the test, which it said had become the judicial standard, "whether to the average person, applying contemporary community standards, the dominant theme of the material taken as a whole appeals to prurient interests." The Court defined obscenity as being "utterly without redeeming social importance" and declared that it is not protected by the First Amendment guarantees.

A Book Named "John Cleland's Memoirs of a Woman of Pleasure (Fanny Hill)" v. Attorney General of Massachusetts (1966). Reversed a state court's decision which had banned a book as prurient and offensive, but said it might have "some minimal literary value." The Court held that a publication could be banned only if all three of these elements are present: (1) the dominant theme of the material taken as a whole appeals to a prurient interest; (2) the material is patently offensive to contemporary community standards; (3) the material is "utterly without redeeming social importance."

Ginzberg v. United States (1966). The Court held that publications produced and advertised solely in order to appeal to prurient interests in sex have the characteristics of illicit merchandise and can not claim the protection of freedom of the press, though in a different marketing context their distribtution might not be challenged.

BROADCASTING

Burstyn v. Wilson (1952). The Court held that a state may not deny a license to show a motion picture on the ground that it is "sacrilegious," as the New York Board of Regents had found Rossellini's *The Miracle* to be. The Court stated that motion pictures are "a significant medium for the communication of ideas" and for the first time brought them under protection of the First Amendment.

Estes v. Texas (1965). Reversed the conviction for swindling of Billie Sol Estes because at the preliminary hearing, and to a lesser degree at the trial, the numerous strands of television cable in the courtroom, the bright lights, and the distracting activities of representatives of news media had prevented a "sober search for the truth" and so had denied Estes a fair trial.

FREEDOM OF RELIGION

Pierce v. Society of Sisters (1925). Invalidated an Oregon law which required parents to send their children to public schools until they had completed the eighth grade, thus preventing their attendance at accredited parochial and other private schools. The Court held that the law violated the Fourteenth Amendment (*a*) by unreasonably interfering with the liberty of parents to direct the upbringing and education of their children and (*b*) by depriving parochial schools of their property and business without due process of law.

Cantwell v. Connecticut (1940). The Court held for the first time that the due-process clause of the Fourteenth Amendment applies to the states the First Amendment's guarantees of religious freedom, including an absolute freedom of belief and a qualified freedom of action. In reversing the convictions, under Connecticut law, of three Jehovah's Witnesses, the Court declared that a permit is not necessary for an effort to proselytize on the streets; nor did a breach of the peace result from the playing of a phonograph record which attacked another religious faith.

Flag-Salute Cases (1940, 1943). Two cases, *Minersville School District* v. *Gobitis* (1940) and *West Virginia State Board of Education* v. *Barnette* (1943). They involved the power of state authorities to exclude children from the public schools for their refusal, on religious grounds, to salute the American flag during school exercises. In the first case, the Court supported a state's requirement of a salute as a means of inculcating the children's loyalty to an orderly political society, holding that such requirement did not interfere with religious freedom. In the second case, only three years later, the earlier decision was overruled. The Court declared that any official effort to prescribe orthodoxy in politics or religion, or to force citizens against their will formally to profess adherence to such orthodoxy, is a violation of the Fourteenth Amendment, which incorporates the substance of the First.

Everson v. Board of Education (1947). The Court upheld the public payment of the cost of transporting children to religious schools as a means by which parents can "get their children, regardless of their religion, safely and expeditiously to and from accredited schools." The Court recognized the "wall between church and state" but held that it had not been breached by this decision.

McCollum v. Board of Education (1948). The Court held that the school authorities of Champaign, Illinois, had infringed the "establishment of religion" clause of the Constitution when they allowed representatives of Catholic, Jewish, and Protestant faiths to give religious instruction on school property during school hours, although the school authorities did not pay for the religious instruction and enforced the attendance of only those children whose parents entered the program. The Court held that the tax-supported schools were being used to disseminate religious doctrines and the compulsory education law was being used to promote sectarian causes. The program was thus inconsistent with the First and Fourteenth Amendments.

Zorach v. Clauson (1952). Upheld New York City's public school, released-time religious education program, which allowed students, at the written request of parents, to secure religious instruction during school hours on premises other than school property. Construing the separation and establishment clauses of the First Amendment less narrowly than in *McCollum* v. *Board of Education,* the Court held that the authors of those clauses never intended to establish an absolute separation of church and state and that absolute separation would be impracticable and contrary to the tenets of a people whose institutions presuppose a Supreme Being.

Engel v. Vitale (1962). Invalidated the use in public schools of a prayer (the so-called Regents' Prayer) as part of its official function of supervising the schools. The Court said that the prescribing of a prayer violated the First Amendment's prohibition of laws establishing a religion, a restriction which applies to the states through the due-process clause of the Fourteenth Amendment.

School District of Abington Township v. Schempp (1963). Held that recitation of the Lord's Prayer or reading from the Bible during opening school exercises violates the First Amendment. The Court declared that the Constitution requires a "wholesome neutrality" between church and state "that neither advances nor inhibits religion"; but, the Court added, this does not establish secularism or prevent objective study in the public schools of the Bible or of religions.

Board of Education v. Allen (1968). Approved New York State's program of lending secular textbooks to children attending parochial schools because (*a*) the books, though selected by the school, are furnished at the request of the pupil and remain at least technically the property of the state; (*b*) no funds are given to parochial schools —the financial benefit is to children and their parents—and (*c*) the people's continued willingness to rely partly on private and parochial schools indicates that a wide segment of the public believes that such schools perform an acceptable function.

Walz v. Tax Commission of the City of New York (1970). A taxpayer's suit (*cf. Flast* v. *Cohen under* The Spending Power, page 77) designed to test a state law granting to churches a property-tax exemption on land used exclusively for religious purposes. The Court said that (*a*) such an exemption is not in violation of the First Amendment; it is rather an evidence of the state's benevolent neutrality toward religion, so long as no sect or denomination is favored over others and none suffers interference; (*b*) such exemption does not inhibit the activities of other organizations that contribute to the moral improvement of the community; and (*c*) it creates only a minimal and remote involvement between church and state—far less than assessment and taxation of church property would create.

Lemon v. Kurtzman (1971). Declared unconstitutional, as in violation of the First and Fourteenth Amendments, laws of Pennsylvania and Rhode Island which granted funds to religious schools (or supplemented salaries paid by such schools) for training solely in non-religious subjects. The Court held (*a*) that elementary and high-school teaching in religious schools is closely involved with religious indoctrination; (*b*) that state inspection and evaluation to differentiate between religious and secular content of education in religious schools is fraught with the sort of entanglement which the Constitution forbids; and (*c*) that "the divisive political potential" of pressures for and against state aid to parochial schools is an "evil" which the First Amendment sought to avoid.

Tilton v. Richardson (1971). The Court upheld, five to four, an Act of Congress, 1963, which granted federal aid in the construction of academic buildings on campuses of church-related and other private colleges. The Court reasoned that college students are "less impressionable and less susceptible to religious indoctrination" than younger students, and that a one-time, single-purpose construction grant causes few entanglements between church and state. However, the Court invalidated one provision of the law which would have allowed religious use of the buildings after twenty years.

UNREASONABLE SEARCHES AND SEIZURES

Olmstead v. United States (1928). The Court ruled that federal government agents did not violate the prohibition against unreasonable searches and seizures when, without actually entering a person's premises, they obtained evidence against him by tapping his telephone wire. (Six years later the Federal Communications Act prohibited anyone not authorized by the sender from wiretapping or publishing the substance of any intercepted communication, but federal prosecuting officers continued to use evidence obtained by state wiretapping.)

Mapp v. Ohio (1961). The Court held that evidence secured without an authenticated search warrant, which would be excluded in a federal prosecution, must be excluded in a state prosecution (in this instance for possession of pornographic material), since the procedural standards under the unreasonable-search-and-seizure clause of the Fourth Amendment are included in the Fourteenth Amendment's guarantee of due process.

Katz v. United States (1967). Reversed *Olmstead* v. *United States* and brought electronic surveillance within the purview of the Fourth Amendment's prohibition of unreasonable searches and seizures. In this case the listening device was hidden in the top of a glass-enclosed public telephone booth often used by a suspected bookmaker, and the police listened only when the suspect was in the booth. The Court held that a conversation was a "thing" that could be seized, and so the police had violated the suspect's privacy, but that if they had first obtained a warrant, their search would have been within the limits of the Fourth Amendment.

Terry v. Ohio (1968). Upheld a "stop-and-frisk" law. The Court said that when an experienced police officer observes unusual conduct which leads him to believe that a crime is about to be committed, after identifying himself as a policeman, he may "frisk," or gently pat down the outer clothing of, a suspected person, and if he finds dangerous weapons, they are admissable as evidence.

United States v. United States District Court for the Eastern District of Michigan (1972). Declared unconstitutional a long-continued government practice of tapping, without prior court approval, the telephone wires of individuals who have no significant connection with a foreign power but who are suspected of domestic subversion. The Court held that "Fourth Amendment freedoms cannot properly be guaranteed if domestic surveillance may be conducted solely within the discretion of the executive branch. . . . Nor must the fear of unauthorized official eavesdropping deter vigorous citizen dissent and discussion of Government action in private conversation."

SELF-INCRIMINATION

Twining v. New Jersey (1908). The Court held that exemption from compulsory self-incrimination in a criminal proceeding is neither an immunity of national citizenship guaranteed against abridgement by the states under the Fourteenth Amendment nor an exemption required of the states by the standards of due process. Overruled in 1964 by *Malloy* v. *Hogan* (see page 112).

Chambers v. Florida (1940). The Court held that due process of law was denied when the police obtained "sunrise confessions" from four Negroes after they had been questioned for five days in the absence of friends, advisers, or counsel and "under circumstances calculated to break the strongest nerves and the stoutest resistance."

Adamson v. California (1947). The Court held that a California statute permitting judicial comment on the failure of a defendant to take the stand did not violate the Fifth Amendment's prohibition of self-incrimination and, in essence, reiterated earlier rulings, such as *Twining* v. *New Jersey* and *Palko* v. *Connecticut,* that the due-process clause of the Fourteenth Amendment did not extend to state courts the procedural limitations of the Bill of Rights. Overruled by *Malloy* v. *Hogan* (see below).

Ullmann v. United States (1956). The Court upheld the constitutionality of a 1954 Act of Congress under which immunity from criminal prosecution could be granted to persons whose testimony was required by Congressional committees in national security matters. The Court declared that a person can be compelled to testify under such immunity even though such disabilities as loss of a job, denial of a passport, or public opprobrium might result, because the Fifth Amendment's protection against compulsory self-incrimination applies only to criminal proceedings.

Slochower v. Board of Higher Education (1956). Invalidated the discharge under a New York City ordinance of a tenured professor in a municipal college because the professor had invoked the Fifth Amendment's guarantee against self-incrimination in a congressional investigation into Communist activity. The Court held that invocation of the self-incrimination clause of the Fifth Amendment is a procedural protection for the individual and a constitutional right, and does not imply, *ipso facto,* any violation of law or professional incompetence; automatic dismissal as in this case was therefore a violation of the Fourteenth Amendment's due-process clause.

Mallory v. United States (1957). The Court held that a confession was invalid as evidence because it had been obtained from a defendant while he was being detained by arresting officers for an unduly long time (about eighteen hours) before being brought before a committing magistrate. See *Escobedo* v. *Illinois* and *Miranda* v. *Arizona,* page 117.

Malloy v. Hogan (1964). Reversed a state judge's citation for contempt of a witness who refused to answer questions on the ground that his answers might incriminate him. The effect was to overrule *Twining* v. *New Jersey* and *Adamson* v. *California* and to extend by the Fourteenth Amendment the protection of the Fifth Amendment against self-incrimination. The Court declared that it would be "incongruous to have different standards determine the validity of a claim of privilege," depending on "whether the claim was asserted in a state or a federal court," and ruled that the federal standard should prevail.

Albertson v. Subversive Activities Control Board (1965). The Court declared that provisions of the Internal Security Act and other laws requiring individual Communists to register were void under the self-incrimination clause of the Fifth Amendment, because admission of Communist affiliation would expose the registrant to criminal prosecution. This decision rendered practically inoperative provisions of other laws requiring the registration of the Communist party and Communist-front organizations.

Zicarelli v. New Jersey State Committee of Investigation (1972). Upheld a sentence, for contempt of court, of a witness who refused to testify before the Commission when state laws provided that neither the testimony given nor leads derived from it could be used in subsequent prosecutions. The Court held that the prohibition against compulsory self-incrimination had not been breached because the witness was left in the same position as if he had remained silent. He can later be prosecuted on evidence "derived from a legitimate source wholly independent of the compelled testimony."

DOUBLE JEOPARDY

Palko v. Connecticut (1937). Sustained the right of a state to appeal in a criminal case to a higher court. The law of Connecticut permitted such an appeal upon questions of law. Palko, after having been convicted of second-degree murder, was retried, convicted of first-degree murder, and sentenced to death. The Court, through Justice Cardozo, distinguished between the procedural guarantees of the Bill of Rights and the First Amendment freedoms which had been "absorbed" into the Fourteenth Amendment; the First Amendment freedoms were "implicit in a scheme of ordered liberty," but the procedural rights were not of "the very essence" of liberty. Justice could still be done without jury trial or freedom from compulsory self-incrimination or from double jeopardy. In this case all that the state asked was "a trial free from the corrosion of substantial legal error." (Overruled by *Benton* v. *Maryland,* see page 114).

Louisiana ex rel. Francis v. Resweber (1947). A convicted murderer who had escaped death due to mechanical failure of the electric chair sought to prevent a second attempt at execution on the grounds of double jeopardy and cruel and unusual punishment. The Court held, five to four, that Louisiana was not violating these standards in proceeding a second time to carry out sentence of death by electrocution.

Bartkus v. Illinois (1959). The Court, five to four, reiterated its position that the due-process clause of the Fourteenth Amendment does not apply all the express limitations of the Bill of Rights to state jurisdictions. In this case, conviction for an offense (robbery of a federally insured loan association) in a state court after the defendant had been acquitted of the same offense in a federal court was held not to violate due process or to raise any valid question of double jeopardy.

Benton v. Maryland (1969). Overruled *Palko* v. *Connecticut* and incorporated the Fifth Amendment's guarantee against double jeopardy into the Fourteenth Amendment. The case was one in which on first trial for burglary and larceny, the defendant had been convicted of burglary but acquitted of larceny. On second trial (held because of errors in the conviction for burglary) he had been convicted of both burglary and larceny. The Court held that the conviction for larceny had been obtained after the defendant had been subjected to jeopardy a second time, in violation of the Fifth Amendment.

TRIAL BY JURY

Strauder v. West Virginia (1880). Declared unconstitutional a West Virginia statute requiring that jury lists be made up entirely of white male citizens, on the ground that the statute violated the rights of Negroes under the equal-protection clause of the Fourteenth Amendment and deprived them of due process of law.

Hurtado v. California (1884). The Court ruled that the protection of life and liberty of the person afforded by the due-process clause of the Fourteenth Amendment does not require a state to use an indictment or presentment of a grand jury in prosecutions for murder or other offenses. The state, after examining and committing the accused through a magistrate's court, may substitute for indictment or presentment, an information certifying "probable guilt."

Maxwell v. Dow (1900). Affirmed the judgment of a Utah court in which the jury was composed of eight persons, as permitted by state law, instead of twelve, as required in federal courts. The Court held that trial by a jury of twelve was not one of the privileges and immunities of citizens of the United States guaranteed against impairment by state courts.

Patton v. United States (1930). Sustained a verdict arrived at in a lower federal court by eleven jurors after the twelfth juror had become ill and the defense and the prosecution had agreed to proceed without him. The defendant later claimed that the jury was an instrument of government and not subject to alteration. However, the Court held that it was rather a valuable privilege for the protection of the accused; and since a defendant could, by a confession, waive a jury trial altogether, his consent to trial by eleven jurors was equally valid. The Court maintained the rule that without such a waiver, trial by jury in federal courts must be by twelve persons; that the trial must be under the superintendence of a judge; and that the verdict must be unanimous.

Norris v. Alabama (Second Scottsboro Case, 1935). Reversed the conviction of a Negro youth for rape because of a "long-continued, unvarying and wholesale exclusion of Negroes from jury service" in the county in which the trial occurred. Going behind the record in the case, the Court found that no Negroes had ever been called for duty in the state court, and from this concluded that no Negroes' names had ever been inserted in the jury wheel, though many Negro residents were qualified for jury duty and some had served on juries in federal courts.

Duncan v. Louisiana (1968). Reversed the conviction in magistrate's court without a jury for an offense for which the maximum sentence was two years in prison, though Duncan's sentence was only sixty days. The Court declared that any offense with such a maximum penalty was not a petty crime and that the right of jury trial prevails in state courts in criminal cases which if tried in federal courts, would be tried by jury. This was the first case in which the requirement of a jury trial was incorporated in the Fourteenth Amendment's guarantee of due process.

United States v. Jackson (1968). Declared unconstitutional a provision of the Federal Kidnapping Act that authorized a jury to impose the death penalty if the kidnapper had harmed his victim. The Court said that the provision would require a defendant to risk his life in order to obtain a jury trial.

Witherspoon v. Illinois (1968). The Court prohibited the death sentence when the jury which had imposed or recommended it had been chosen after screening out prospective jurors who had expressed conscientious or religious scruples against capital punishment.

CRUEL AND UNUSUAL PUNISHMENT

Louisiana ex rel. Francis v. Resweber (1947). *See under* Double Jeopardy, page 113.

Trop v. Dulles (1958). The Court declared unconstitutional, as a cruel and unusual punishment forbidden by the Eighth Amendment, a provision of the Nationality Act of 1940 which automatically took away American citizenship from members of the armed forces who were convicted of desertion in time of war.

Furman v. Georgia (1972). The Court held, five to four, that the discretionary imposition of the death penalty, so infrequently and randomly imposed that it was no longer a credible deterrent from crime, constituted a cruel and unusual punishment in violation of the Eighth and Fourteenth Amendments. Each Justice delivered a separate opinion. Those in the majority said: the death penalty has in fact been imposed on a capriciously selected handful (Stewart); it is uniquely degrading and is tolerated only because of its disuse (Brennan); legislative policy loses much of its force when broad delegation to impose the death penalty is vested in judges and juries (White); the death penalty falls on the poor and members of minority groups who cannot afford to employ competent counsel (Marshall); and judges should see to it that general laws are not applied spottily (Douglas). The minority Justices disagreed about the value of the death penalty, but all said that, if abolished, abolition should be by legislative act, and not by the Court.

RIGHT OF COUNSEL

Powell v. Alabama (First Scottsboro Case, 1932). Reversed an Alabama court's conviction of a Negro youth for rape, on the ground that the trial judge had not made effective provision for counsel for his defense. No appointment of counsel had been made until the morning of the trial, when there was no time to prepare a defense. The Court declared that "the right to be heard would be, in many cases, of little avail if it did not comprehend the right to be heard by counsel. . . . The failure of the trial court to make an effective appointment of counsel was a denial of due process within the meaning of the Fourteenth Amendment."

Johnson v. Zerbst (1938). Reversed the conviction, for forgery, of a young marine who had informed the federal district judge that he had no counsel but was ready for trial and, through ignorance of the law, had failed to assert important rights while attempting to act as his own counsel. The Court held that an accused person may waive his right to counsel, but the waiver must be clearly and intelligently made (as it was not in this case); and that the trial judge has the "serious and weighty responsibility . . . of determining whether there is an intelligent and competent waiver by the accused."

Gideon v. Wainwright (1963). The Court included among the fundamental rights guaranteed by the Fourteenth Amendment the right under the Sixth Amendment to be represented by counsel when being tried for any crime in a state court; and the Court held that this includes the right of an indigent defendant to have counsel assigned by the state court.

Escobedo v. Illinois (1964). The Court held that the refusal of police to honor an accused's request to consult an attorney, their obtaining a confession from him after failing to advise him of his rights, and the admission of the confession as evidence by a state court constituted a denial of due process. (*Cf. Miranda v. Arizona.*)

Miranda v. Arizona (1966). The Court extended the protections of the Fifth and Fourteenth Amendments by holding that a suspect in the hands of police authorities must be clearly informed *prior* to any questioning that he has the right to remain silent and that anything he says can be used against him in a court of law; that he has the right to the presence of an attorney; and that if he cannot afford an attorney, one must be appointed for him.

Harris v. New York (1971). The Court held, five to four, that statements made to the police by a prisoner who had not been informed of his rights to silence and to counsel, though inadmissible as direct evidence, can be used to contradict statements by the prisoner when he testifies in his own behalf in court. The ruling in *Miranda v. Arizona* "can not be perverted into a license to use perjury"; and the advantage of exposing false testimony outweighs the "speculative possibility that impermissible police conduct will be encouraged."

Argerdinger v. Hamlin (1972). Extended the right of counsel to all cases in which the judge or magistrate wishes to preserve his option of imposing a jail sentence. The Court held that no indigent person can be sentenced to jail "without a knowing and intelligent waiver of his right" to counsel or unless he has been provided by the court with the free services of a lawyer.

THIRTEENTH AMENDMENT

Bailey v. Alabama (1911). Invalidated, as in violation of the Thirteenth Amendment, an Alabama statute which made it a criminal offense to obtain an advance payment on wages with intent to defraud the employer. The Court held that the inevitable effect of the statute was to expose to criminal penalties any person who failed or refused to perform a contract for personal services in order to liquidate a debt; and that, judging its purpose by its effect, it sought to provide a way to compel the performance of personal service.

Pollock v. Williams (1944). The Court held that the Thirteenth Amendment prohibits all legislation which would compel a person to work in order to pay off a debt; a state may not "directly or indirectly command involuntary servitude even if it was voluntarily contracted for."

Jones v. Alfred H. Mayer Co. (1968). Sustained an Act of Congress, passed in 1866, which prohibited both public and private racial discrimination in the sale or rental of property. The law had not previously been enforced, and similar civil rights legislation had been declared unconstitutional in 1883 (*see* Civil Rights Cases, page 122). Justice Stewart, for the Court, said that the Thirteenth Amendment was intended to remove badges of slavery from the United States. "When racial discrimination herds men into ghettos and makes their ability to buy property turn on the color of their skins, then it too is a relic of slavery. The Thirteenth Amendment includes the right to buy whatever a white man can buy, the right to live wherever a white man can live."

FOURTEENTH AMENDMENT: CITIZENSHIP

Dred Scott v. Sandford (1857). The case of a Negro slave who had resided with his master for several years in the free state of Illinois and at Fort Snelling, which was in a territory that had been made free by the Missouri Compromise. On being returned to Missouri, Scott sued for his freedom. The Court held that Scott was not a citizen and therefore had no standing in court under the diversity-of-citizenship clause of the Constitution; that national citizenship was determined by state citizenship; and in *obiter dicta,* that the Missouri Compromise was unconstitutional because Congress had no right to prevent citizens from carrying their slaves into a territory or to impair the protection which should be given to property while it is in a territory.

United States v. Wong Kim Ark (1898). The Court declared that a child born in the United States and subject to its jurisdiction is, according to the Fourteenth Amendment, a citizen of the United States, even if his parents are aliens ineligible for naturalization. Certain other children born in the United States, however, are not citizens, because they are not subject to its jurisdiction. These include children of diplomatic (but not consular) representatives of foreign states; children of enemies born during hostile occupation of American soil; children born on foreign public ships in American territorial waters; and Indians born on reservations. Congress later (1924) made all Indians American citizens.

Trop v. Dulles (1958). *See under* Cruel and Unusual Punishment, page 116.

Perez v. Brownell (1958). Upheld (five to four) a provision of the Smith Act (1940) that a native-born American citizen might forfeit his citizenship by participating in an election in a foreign country. The Court reasoned that, under its power to legislate on foreign relations, Congress might act to prevent interference by Americans in the affairs of a foreign country. (Overruled by *Afroyim* v. *Rusk,* see below.)

Schneider v. Rusk (1964). Declared unconstitutional a section of the Immigration and Nationality Act of 1952 which deprived of citizenship a naturalized person who had a continued residence of three years in the country of his birth or prior nationality. Justice Douglas, for the Court, said that to deprive a naturalized citizen of a privilege which a citizen by birth could exercise was equivalent to maintaining a second-class citizenship.

Afroyim v. Rusk (1967). Overruled *Perez* v. *Brownell* and held that Afroyim, who had voted in a national election in Israel, had *not* thereby lost his American citizenship. The Court stated that the definition of citizenship in the Fourteenth Amendment is binding on Congress and that it prevents "forcible destruction" or deprivation of citizenship without the individual's consent.

PRIVILEGES AND IMMUNITIES OF CITIZENS

Crandall v. Nevada (1867). Invalidated a Nevada tax on the transportation of passengers out of the state on the ground that it obstructed a person's constitutional privilege "to come to the seat of
his government . . . and to transact any business he may have with
it, to seek its protection, to share its offices, to engage in administering
its functions. He has the right of free access to its seaports . . . to
the sub-treasuries, land offices, and courts of justice in the several
States."

Slaughter-House Cases (1873). Denied an appeal by butchers of New
Orleans against a state legislative act which, ostensibly to protect
health, gave one company a twenty-five-year monopoly on all slaughtering operations in the city. The Court said that the Fourteenth
Amendment's privileges-and-immunities clause, on which the appel-
lants chiefly relied, had meant, ever since its appearance in the
Articles of Confederation, that one state could not discriminate
against citizens *of other states;* that the Fourteenth Amendment had
defined a national, as distinct from a state, citizenship; and that its
framers had intended it for the protection of Negroes and had never
intended to make Congress the legislature for the "most ordinary
and usual functions" of the states or to make the Supreme Court "a
perpetual censor upon all legislation of the states."

DUE PROCESS UNDER THE FOURTEENTH AMENDMENT

Munn v. Illinois (1877). Sustained state regulation of grain elevator
rates, declaring that the "public has a direct and positive interest"
in private businesses such as that of the operation of grain elevators.
Because it is "clothed with a public interest," property put to such
uses is subject to public control. The case set an important precedent
for judicial support of public regulation of the rates and services of
public utilities.

Fertilizing Company v. Hyde Park (1878). The Court held that a
municipal ordinance forbidding the transportation of offal through
the streets and prohibiting operation of a fertilizer factory within
the city limits was a valid exercise of the police power to suppress
nuisances and protect public health, even though the effect of the
ordinance was to destroy the value of the company's franchise.

Noble State Bank v. Haskell (1911). Upheld a state plan for the compulsory insurance of bank deposits as consistent with the due-process clause of the Fourteenth Amendment. The Court reasoned that the police power extends to all great public needs; that such needs embrace the enforcement of the primary conditions of successful commerce; and that the guarantee of bank deposits, upon which the security of check currency depends, may properly be regarded by a state legislature as a condition of successful commerce.

Meyer v. Nebraska (1923). Invalidated a Nebraska statute which prohibited the teaching of foreign languages in elementary schools and also forbade the teaching of any subject in a language other than English. The Court held that the statute unreasonably infringed on the liberty to teach and the liberty of parents to secure instruction for their children, both liberties being among those protected by the Fourteenth Amendment.

Euclid v. Ambler Realty Co. (1926). Upheld a comprehensive zoning ordinance restricting and regulating the location of businesses, industries, and various types of dwellings. Despite the loss sustained by many property-holders in the zoned areas, the Court held that as a reasonable exercise of the state's police power, the ordinance did not violate due process.

Tyson v. Banton (1927). Invalidated a New York State law limiting the resale price of theater tickets, on the ground that ticket brokerage was not a business affected with a public interest and hence its regulation was not a legitimate exercise of the state's police power.

Nebbia v. New York (1934). Upheld the fixing of minimum and maximum prices of milk by a New York State board. The Court thus expanded beyond the limited category of public utilities the scope of regulation under the police power and virtually abandoned the concept that only "businesses affected with a public interest" were subject to regulation.

STATE LABOR LEGISLATION

Holden v. Hardy (1898). Upheld a state law limiting to eight hours the working day in underground mines and smelters. The Court saw no reason to doubt the legislature's judgment that working long hours at such occupations was detrimental to health. To the argument that the worker's right to contract for his labor was violated by the law, the Court replied that "the state still retains an interest in his welfare, however reckless he may be."

Lochner v. New York (1905). Invalidated a state law limiting the hours of labor in bakeries to ten a day or sixty a week on the grounds that (*a*) state police power was overreached, as the occupation of baker was not dangerous to health; and (*b*) the statute interfered with the rights of individuals and deprived them of freedom of contract, protected by the due-process clause of the Fourteenth Amendment. Overruled by *Bunting* v. *Oregon* (*q.v.*).

Muller v. Oregon (1908). Upheld an Oregon statute forbidding the employment of women in certain industries for more than ten hours in any one day, thus modifying the *Lochner* v. *New York* decision, apparently on the ground that women were less able than men to endure sustained labor and therefore required legislative protection. Louis Brandeis, as counsel for the state, presented a mass of sociological data to buttress the law, and the Court's admission of such evidence set a notable precedent.

Bunting v. Oregon (1917). Sustained the Oregon legislature in establishing a ten-hour day for both men and women, not solely as a health measure but because "in view of the well-known fact that the custom in our industries does not sanction a longer service than ten hours per day, it cannot be held, as a matter of law, that the legislative requirement is unreasonable or arbitrary as to hours of labor." *Cf. Adkins* v. *Children's Hospital* (1923) under Federal Legislation Concerning Labor, page 84.

Wolff Packing Co. v. Court of Industrial Relations (1923). Declared unconstitutional an act of the Kansas legislature which created a Court of Industrial Relations with power to settle disputes in food, fuel, transportation, and certain other industries by mandatory awards on hours and conditions of work and minimum wages. The Court reasoned (*a*) that meat-packing was not affected with a public interest and (*b*) that the statute violated the rights of employer and employee to bargain collectively.

West Coast Hotel Co. v. Parrish (1937). The Court reversed earlier decisions (as in *Adkins* v. *Children's Hospital*) by upholding the constitutionality of state legislation prescribing minimum-wage rates for women. The Court rejected arguments that such legislation violated the due-process clause of the Fourteenth Amendment, stating that "the liberty safeguarded is liberty in a social organization which requires the protection of law against the evils which menace the health, safety, morals and welfare of the people."

EQUAL PROTECTION OF THE LAWS

Civil Rights Cases (1883). The Court held void the Civil Rights Act of 1875, which forbade proprietors of public conveyances, hotels, restaurants, and places of amusement to refuse accommodations to a person on account of his race, color, or previous condition of servitude. The prohibitions of racial discrimination in the equal-protection and due-process clauses of the Fourteenth Amendment were thus confined to state action and were not until the mid-twentieth century extended to invasions of personal rights by individuals.

Barbier v. Connolly (1885). The Court held that a San Francisco ordinance prohibiting the night operation of laundries in certain sections did not contravene the equal-protection clause of the Fourteenth Amendment, because it was a reasonable protection against fire. "The State police power to prescribe regulations to promote the health, peace, morals, education and good order of the people, and to legislate so as to increase the industries of the State, develop its resources, and add to its wealth and prosperity" must often require special legislation for certain districts. Class legislation is prohibited, but special laws "do not furnish just ground for complaint if they operate alike upon all persons and property under the same circumstances and conditions."

Yick Wo v. Hopkins (1886). Invalidated a San Francisco laundry-licensing ordinance on the grounds that it established an arbitrary classification of persons, prohibited by the equal-protection clause of the Fourteenth Amendment, and that the authority conferred by the ordinance had been administered so as to discriminate against Chinese laundrymen.

Plessy v. Ferguson (1896). Upheld a Louisiana law of 1890 which required railroads to provide "separate but equal" accommodations for white and colored passengers. The Court said that a law which recognizes a difference in color "has no tendency to destroy the legal equality of the two races." It added that the Fourteenth Amendment was not intended to enforce "social, as distinguished from political, equality or a commingling of the races upon terms unsatisfactory to either." If the enforced segregation "stamps the colored race with the badge of inferiority," it is solely because "the colored race chooses to put that construction upon it." The elder Justice Harlan's dissent strikingly presaged the Court's opinion in *Brown* v. *Board of Education of Topeka* (1954); see page 125.

Truax v. Raich (1915). Invalidated an Arizona statute which required private employers to hire eighty per cent of their work force from among American citizens. As a result of the law, Raich, an Austrian citizen, had lost his job. The Court held that the statute denied equal protection of the laws; that alien residents are entitled to livelihood; and that state deprivation of their means of livelihood would be equivalent to prohibiting immigration.

Buchanan v. Warley (1917). The Court struck down as a violation of due process affecting property rights under the Fourteenth Amendment a city ordinance which sought to establish residential separation of whites and Negroes by prohibiting a member of one race from occupying premises in districts where a majority of the dwellings were occupied by members of the other race. The decision was circumvented by resort to restrictive covenants, which were later denied judicial enforcement. See *Shelley* v. *Kraemer,* page 124.

Texas Primary Cases (1927–1953). *See under* Primary Elections, page 71.

Morgan v. Virginia (1946). Invalidated a Virginia statute requiring separation of the races on motor carriers on the ground that the law interfered with interstate commerce, causing a disturbance of the comfort of interstate passengers and limiting their freedom to select seats. The Court held that interstate motor carriers required a "single, uniform rule to promote and protect national travel."

Shelley v. Kraemer (1948). Denied judicial enforcement of restrictive covenants (long-term agreements between private parties limiting the right to own or occupy premises to certain races or groups of persons and excluding other races or groups). The Court held that though such voluntary agreements were in themselves legal, their enforcement by state courts violated the equal-protection clause of the Fourteenth Amendment.

EQUAL PROTECTION IN EDUCATION

Missouri ex rel. Gaines v. Canada (1938). Introduced a modification of the "separate but equal" doctrine regarding educational opportunities for Negroes. The Court sustained a Negro's right to a higher professional education on terms of equality with whites by requiring the Negro's admission to the all-white law school of a state university at least until a law school for Negroes had been provided. The state's offer to finance the Negro's legal education at an out-of-state university was explicitly rejected as less than equal treatment.

McLaurin v. Oklahoma State Regents (1950). The case of a Negro who had been admitted as a graduate student to the University of Oklahoma but who, as required by state law, had been segregated from white students by seating assignments in classrooms, library, and cafeteria. The Court held that these segregations denied him the Fourteenth Amendment's guarantee of equal protection because they impaired "his ability to study, to engage in discussions and exchange views with other students, and, in general, to learn his profession."

Sweatt v. Painter (1950). The Court ordered a Negro admitted to the University of Texas law school, from which he had been excluded because of his race, even though Texas had established a new law school for Negroes. The Court went behind the record to determine whether or not the separate facilities were indeed "equal" and found that they were not equal in faculty, course offerings, library facilities, attainments of alumni, or reputation.

Brown v. Board of Education of Topeka (1954, 1955). Outlawed as unconstitutional the segregation of Negro students in the public schools. After reviewing the efforts of various states to satisfy the "separate but equal" interpretation given the Fourteenth Amendment's due-process clause in *Plessy* v. *Ferguson* (*q.v.*), the Court declared that this doctrine in fact resulted in denying equal educational opportunity to Negro children. Separate facilities in education, the Court held, are "inherently unequal," and their continuance by the states would breach the equal-protection clause of the Fourteenth Amendment. The Court requested further argument concerning the relief to be granted; and in 1955 it ordered local authorities to "make a prompt and reasonable start" and instructed the lower courts to "proceed with all deliberate speed" to end segregation in public schools.

Bolling v. Sharpe (1954). A companion case to *Brown* v. *Board of Education of Topeka*. The Court ordered the desegregation of the public schools in the District of Columbia. There being no "equal-protection" clause limiting the federal government, the Court based its decision on the due-process clause of the Fifth Amendment.

Green v. County Board of New Kent County (1969). Disallowed, as "intolerable," a school-board plan to give parents freedom of choice to send their children either to a formerly all-white school or to a formerly all-Negro school, because the plan shifted the responsibility for complying with the *Brown* v. *Board of Education of Topeka* decision from the county board to the parents. Declaring that the "time for mere deliberate speed has run out," the Court said that "the burden on a school board today is to come forward with a plan that promises realistically to work and that promises realistically to work *now*."

Swann v. Charlotte-Mecklenburg County Board of Education (1971). The Court held that the constitutional requirement to desegregate public schools does not mean that each school must reflect the racial composition of a community's school system as a whole. The existence of a few all-white or all-black schools does not of itself prove that segregation exists, but school districts must prove that such instances do not result from attempts to segregate the races. The Court also stated that since bus transportation has for years been an integral part of the school system, desegregation plans cannot be limited to walk-in schools. However, boards of education are not required to make adjustments every year because of the changing racial composition of communities.

QUALIFICATIONS AND POWERS
OF FEDERAL OFFICERS

THE PRESIDENT (Term 4 years)

Qualifications. A natural born citizen. Fourteen years a resident in the United States. At least 35 years of age.

Powers and Duties. Execution of all laws. Makes treaties with advice and consent of Senate. Appoints ambassadors to foreign countries, Judges of the Supreme Court and of the inferior federal courts, and about 17,000 other officers of the national government. Recommends measures to Congress. Convenes extraordinary sessions of Congress. Has veto power over legislation unless repassed by a two-thirds majority. Commander in Chief of the armed forces. Takes office January 20th. Limited to two elective terms and a maximum of ten years in office.

Salary and Allowances. Salary of $200,000 per year. Special taxable allowance of $50,000 for White House and other expenses, plus a maximum of $40,000 (non-taxable) for travel and entertainment.

VICE PRESIDENT (Term 4 years)

Qualifications. Same as for President.

Powers and Duties. Presiding officer of the Senate, with vote only in case of tie. Aids President, when requested, in foreign and domestic matters. Becomes Acting President in cases of presidential disability. Becomes President if President dies or resigns.

Salary and Allowances. Salary of $62,500 per year plus $10,000 per year for expenses.

HOUSE OF REPRESENTATIVES (Term 2 years)
435 Members

Qualifications. At least 25 years of age. An American citizen seven years. Resident of state where elected.

Special Powers and Duties.* Originates revenue bills. Originates and prefers impeachment charges. Elects President if Electoral College fails to do so.

Salary. $42,500 per year.

SENATE (Term 6 years)
Two from each state (100)
One third of the membership elected every two years.

Qualifications. At least 30 years of age. At least nine years a citizen. Must be a resident of the state from which he is elected.

Special Powers and Duties.* Confirms Presidential appointments. Approves or rejects treaties. Acts as court of impeachment. Elects Vice President if Electoral College fails to do so.

Salary. $42,500 per year.

THE CABINET

An extraconstitutional body made up of the heads of the twelve executive departments and other high officers, such as the Vice President and the Director of the Budget, who are invited by the President regularly to meet with him and give him advice.

Department	Date Created	Title of Head
State	July 27, 1789	Secretary of State
Treasury	Sept. 2, 1789	Secretary of the Treasury
Interior	March 3, 1849	Secretary of the Interior
Justice	February 9, 1889	Attorney General
Agriculture	June 22, 1870	Secretary of Agriculture
Commerce	March 4, 1913	Secretary of Commerce
Labor	March 4, 1913	Secretary of Labor
Defense	Sept. 18, 1947	Secretary of Defense

* These obviously do not include the general powers and duties common to both Houses of Congress, e.g., the power to lay and collect taxes and to appropriate money, etc.

Health, Education, and Welfare	April 1, 1953	Secretary of Health, Education, and Welfare
Housing and Urban Development	Sept. 9, 1965	Secretary of Housing and Urban Development
Transportation	Oct. 15, 1966	Secretary of Transportation

A single Department of Commerce and Labor had been established on February 14, 1903, but in 1913 two separate departments were created. The Department of the Army (formerly the War Department, established in 1789) and the Department of the Navy (established in 1798) were organized under the National Military Establishment in 1947 (name changed to Department of Defense in 1949). The Secretaries of the separate armed services were deprived of Cabinet rank in 1947. The Post Office Department, created in 1829, was abolished by Act of Congress, August 12, 1970, and replaced by an independent publicly owned corporation. The Postmaster General was removed from the Cabinet and from the line of succession to the Presidency.

SUCCESSION TO THE PRESIDENCY

The Vice President is the constitutional successor to the President. To provide for succession in case of the death, resignation, or disability of both the President and the Vice President, a law of Congress in 1792 put the President pro tempore of the Senate and the Speaker of the House, in that order, next in line of succession. In 1886 this law was repealed and the succession devolved upon the heads of the executive departments nearly in the order of their creation. In 1947 Congress again changed the order of succession by placing the Speaker of the House and the President pro tem of the Senate immediately after the Vice President and before the heads of departments. The present order of succession for heads of departments is: Secretaries of State, the Treasury, and Defense, the Attorney General, and the Secretaries of the Interior, Agriculture, Commerce, Labor, of Health, Education and Welfare, of Housing and Urban Development, and of Transportation. The likelihood that any legislative or Cabinet member will succeed to the presidency has been greatly reduced by the adoption of the Twenty-fifth Amendment.

CHARTS AND TABLES

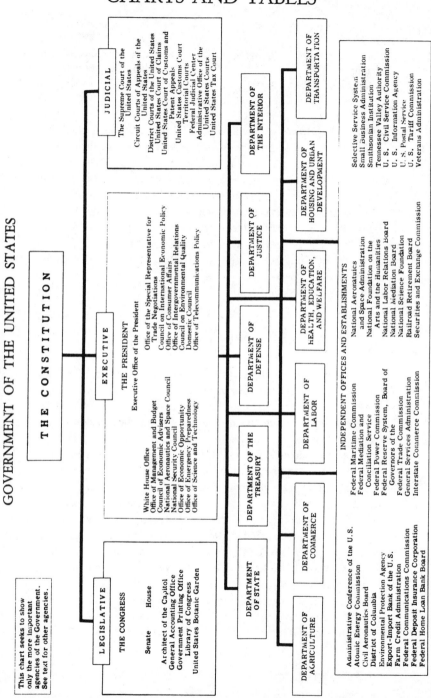

GOVERNMENT OF THE UNITED STATES

This chart seeks to show only the more important agencies of the Government. See text for other agencies.

THE CONSTITUTION

LEGISLATIVE

THE CONGRESS

Senate   House

Architect of the Capitol
General Accounting Office
Government Printing Office
Library of Congress
United States Botanic Garden

EXECUTIVE

THE PRESIDENT

Executive Office of the President

White House Office
Office of Management and Budget
Council of Economic Advisers
National Aeronautics and Space Council
National Security Council
Office of Economic Opportunity
Office of Emergency Preparedness
Office of Science and Technology

Office of the Special Representative for Trade Negotiations
Council on International Economic Policy
Office of Consumer Affairs
Office of Intergovernmental Relations
Council on Environmental Quality
Domestic Council
Office of Telecommunications Policy

JUDICIAL

The Supreme Court of the United States
Circuit Courts of Appeals of the United States
District Courts of the United States
United States Court of Claims
United States Court of Customs and Patent Appeals
United States Customs Court
Territorial Courts
Federal Judicial Center
Administrative Office of the United States Courts
United States Tax Court

DEPARTMENT OF AGRICULTURE

DEPARTMENT OF STATE

DEPARTMENT OF COMMERCE

DEPARTMENT OF THE TREASURY

DEPARTMENT OF LABOR

DEPARTMENT OF DEFENSE

DEPARTMENT OF HEALTH, EDUCATION, AND WELFARE

DEPARTMENT OF JUSTICE

DEPARTMENT OF HOUSING AND URBAN DEVELOPMENT

DEPARTMENT OF THE INTERIOR

DEPARTMENT OF TRANSPORTATION

INDEPENDENT OFFICES AND ESTABLISHMENTS

Administrative Conference of the U.S.
Atomic Energy Commission
Civil Aeronautics Board
District of Columbia
Environmental Protection Agency
Export-Import Bank of the U.S.
Farm Credit Administration
Federal Communications Commission
Federal Deposit Insurance Corporation
Federal Home Loan Bank Board

Federal Maritime Commission
Federal Mediation and Conciliation Service
Federal Power Commission
Federal Reserve System, Board of Governors of the
Federal Trade Commission
General Services Administration
Interstate Commerce Commission

National Aeronautics and Space Administration
National Foundation on the Arts and the Humanities
National Labor Relations Board
National Mediation Board
National Science Foundation
Railroad Retirement Board
Securities and Exchange Commission

Selective Service System
Small Business Administration
Smithsonian Institution
Tennessee Valley Authority
U. S. Civil Service Commission
U. S. Information Agency
U. S. Postal Service
U. S. Tariff Commission
Veterans Administration

ENTRANCE OF STATES INTO UNION

Original thirteen states indicated by italics.

State	Settled	Area Sq. Mi.	Entered Union
Alabama	1702	51,998	1819
Alaska	1783	586,400	1958
Arizona	1580	113,956	1912
Arkansas	1785	53,335	1836
California	1769	158,297	1850
Colorado	1858	103,948	1876
Connecticut	1635	4,965	1788
Delaware	1638	2,370	1787
Florida	1565	58,666	1845
Georgia	1733	59,265	1788
Hawaii	c500	6,449	1890
Idaho	1842	83,354	1959
Illinois	1720	56,043	1818
Indiana	1733	36,045	1816
Iowa	1788	55,586	1846
Kansas	1827	81,774	1861
Kentucky	1775	40,181	1792
Louisiana	1699	45,409	1812
Maine	1624	29,895	1820
Maryland	1634	9,941	1788
Massachusetts	1620	8,039	1788
Michigan	1668	57,480	1837
Minnesota	1805	80,858	1858
Mississippi	1699	46,362	1817
Missouri	1764	68,727	1821
Montana	1809	146,131	1889
Nebraska	1847	76,808	1867
Nevada	1850	110,690	1864
New Hampshire	1623	9,031	1788

State	Settled	Area Sq. Mi.	Entered Union
New Jersey	1618	7,514	1787
New Mexico	1598	122,503	1912
New York	1614	47,654	1788
North Carolina	1650	48,740	1789
North Dakota	1780	70,183	1889
Ohio	1788	40,740	1803
Oklahoma	1889	69,414	1907
Oregon	1838	95,607	1859
Pennsylvania	1682	45,126	1787
Rhode Island	1636	1,067	1790
South Carolina	1670	30,495	1788
South Dakota	1794	76,868	1889
Tennessee	1757	41,687	1796
Texas	1686	262,398	1845
Utah	1847	82,184	1896
Vermont	1724	9,124	1791
Virginia	1607	40,262	1788
Washington	1845	66,836	1889
West Virginia	1727	24,022	1863
Wisconsin	1670	55,256	1848
Wyoming	1834	97,548	1890

TERRITORIES AND DEPENDENCIES

	Acquired	Area Sq. Mi.
American Samoa	1899—U.S. claims recognized by Germany and Great Britain in treaty	76
Canal Zone	1904—Leased in perpetuity from Panama	553
Guam	1899—ceded to U.S. by Spain	206
Puerto Rico	1899—ceded to U.S. by Spain	3,435
Virgin Islands	1917—purchased from Denmark	133
Wake, Midway, and other Pacific Islands		42

PRESIDENTS OF THE UNITED STATES

No.	Name	Native State	Party	Term
1	GEORGE WASHINGTON (1732–1799)	Va.	Federalist	1789–1797
2	JOHN ADAMS (1735–1826)	Mass.	Federalist	1797–1801
3	THOMAS JEFFERSON (1743–1826)	Va.	Rep.-Dem.	1801–1809
4	JAMES MADISON (1751–1836)	Va.	Rep.-Dem.	1809–1817
5	JAMES MONROE (1758–1831)	Va.	Rep.-Dem.	1817–1825
6	JOHN QUINCY ADAMS (1767–1848)	Mass.	Rep.-Dem.	1825–1829
7	ANDREW JACKSON (1767–1845)	S.C.	Democrat	1829–1837
8	MARTIN VAN BUREN (1782–1862)	N.Y.	Democrat	1837–1841
9	WILLIAM HENRY HARRISON (1773–1841)	Va.	Whig	1841
10	JOHN TYLER (1790–1862)	Va.	Democrat	1841–1845
11	JAMES KNOX POLK (1795–1849)	N.C.	Democrat	1845–1849
12	ZACHARY TAYLOR (1784–1850)	Va.	Whig	1849–1850
13	MILLARD FILLMORE (1800–1874)	N.Y.	Whig	1850–1853
14	FRANKLIN PIERCE (1804–1869)	N.H.	Democrat	1853–1857
15	JAMES BUCHANAN (1791–1868)	Pa.	Democrat	1857–1861
16	ABRAHAM LINCOLN (1809–1865)	Ky.	Republican	1861–1865
17	ANDREW JOHNSON (1808–1875)	N.C.	Republican	1865–1869

No.	Name	Native State	Party	Term
18	ULYSSES S. GRANT (*1822–1885*)	Ohio	Republican	1869–1877
19	RUTHERFORD B. HAYES (*1822–1893*)	Ohio	Republican	1877–1881
20	JAMES A. GARFIELD (*1831–1881*)	Ohio	Republican	1881
21	CHESTER A. ARTHUR (*1830–1886*)	Vt.	Republican	1881–1885
22	GROVER CLEVELAND (*1837–1908*)	N.J.	Democrat	1885–1889
23	BENJAMIN HARRISON (*1833–1901*)	Ohio	Republican	1889–1893
24	GROVER CLEVELAND (*1837–1908*)	N.J.	Democrat	1893–1897
25	WILLIAM McKINLEY (*1843–1901*)	Ohio	Republican	1897–1901
26	THEODORE ROOSEVELT (*1858–1919*)	N.Y.	Republican	1901–1909
27	WILLIAM H. TAFT (*1857–1930*)	Ohio	Republican	1909–1913
28	WOODROW WILSON (*1856–1924*)	Va.	Democrat	1913–1921
29	WARREN G. HARDING (*1865–1923*)	Ohio	Republican	1921–1923
30	CALVIN COOLIDGE (*1872–1933*)	Vt.	Republican	1923–1929
31	HERBERT C. HOOVER (*1874–1964*)	Iowa	Republican	1929–1933
32	FRANKLIN D. ROOSEVELT (*1882–1945*)	N.Y.	Democrat	1933–1945
33	HARRY S TRUMAN (*1884– *)	Mo.	Democrat	1945–1953
34	DWIGHT D. EISENHOWER (*1890–1969*)	Texas	Republican	1953–1961
35	JOHN F. KENNEDY (*1917–1963*)	Mass.	Democrat	1961–1963
36	LYNDON B. JOHNSON (*1908– *)	Texas	Democrat	1963–1969
37	RICHARD M. NIXON (*1913– *)	Calif.	Republican	1969–

JUDICIAL ORGANIZATION OF THE UNITED STATES

Supreme Court. Final jurisdiction over all cases arising in lower federal courts; over cases involving federal questions, from highest state court having jurisdiction to hear the case.

Courts of Appeals. 10 in numbered districts into which the United States (except the District of Columbia) is divided, 1 in the District of Columbia.

> Final jurisdiction over cases arising in federal courts except those heard by the Supreme Court. In addition, the District of Columbia court of appeals has jurisdiction to review determinations of quasi-judicial federal commissions and cases arising in the District which in a state would be decided by the highest state court.

District Courts. 88 courts at least 1 in every state, 1 in Puerto Rico, 1 in the District of Columbia.

> Original jurisdiction over cases arising under United States law.
>
> In addition, the Puerto Rico district court determines some matters arising under local law.
>
> In addition, the District of Columbia district court hears cases which in a state would be decided by the lower state courts of record.

Special Courts. A. Created under Article I, later given status of Article III courts, at least as to salary and tenure of judges:

> Court of Claims
>
> Court of Customs and Patent Appeals hears cases appealed from the Customs Court, Patent Office, and Tariff Commission.
>
> Customs Court

> B. Created under Article I:
>
> Tax Court
>
> Court of Military Appeals

C. Created under Article IV:

Local courts for Puerto Rico with jurisdiction over cases arising under local laws.

District courts in
  Canal Zone
  Virgin Islands
  Guam

with jurisdiction over cases arising both under general United States and under local laws.

SUPREME COURT JUSTICES
SINCE 1789

The Supreme Court first consisted of a Chief Justice and five Associate Justices (*Judiciary Act of 1789*). The number of Associate Justices was reduced to four in 1801, increased to six in 1807, to eight in 1837, to nine in 1863, and reduced to six in 1866. The Act of 1869 provided for a Chief Justice and eight Associate Justices. This number has remained unchanged. Their term of office is for life unless a Judge shall resign or be convicted on impeachment. It is interesting to note that in the entire history of the Supreme Court the only Justice (Samuel Chase) impeached was acquitted.

Name	*State*	*Term*
(**Boldface denotes Chief Justices**)		
John Jay (1745–1829)	New York	1789–1795
John Rutledge (1739–1800)	South Carolina	1789–1791
William Cushing (1732–1810)	Massachusetts	1789–**1810**
James Wilson (1742–1798)	Pennsylvania	1789–1798
John Blair (1732–1800)	Virginia	1789–1796
Robert H. Harrison (1745–1790)	Maryland	1789–1790
James Iredell (1751–1799)	North Carolina	1790–1799
Thomas Johnson (1732–1819)	Maryland	1791–1793
William Paterson (1745–1806)	New Jersey	1793–1806
John Rutledge (1739–1800)	South Carolina	*1795
Samuel Chase (1741–1811)	Maryland	1796–1811
Oliver Ellsworth (1745–1807)	Connecticut	1796–1799
Bushrod Washington (1762–1829)	Virginia	1798–1829
Alfred Moore (1755–1810)	North Carolina	1799–1804
John Marshall (1755–1835)	Virginia	1801–1835
William Johnson (1771–1834)	South Carolina	1804–1834
Brockholst Livingston (1757–1823)	New York	1806–1823
Thomas Todd (1765–1826)	Kentucky	1807–1826
Joseph Story (1779–1845)	Massachusetts	1811–1845
Gabriel Duval (1752–1844)	Maryland	1812–1835
Smith Thompson (1768–1843)	New York	1823–1843

* Senate rejected his appointment Dec. 15, 1795.

Name	State	Term
Robert Trimble (1777–1828)	Kentucky	1826–1828
John McLean (1785–1861)	Ohio	1829–1861
Henry Baldwin (1780–1844)	Pennsylvania	1830–1844
James M. Wayne (1790–1867)	Georgia	1835–1867
Roger B. Taney (1777–1864)	Maryland	1836–1864
Philip P. Barbour (1783–1841)	Virginia	1836–1841
John Catron (1786–1865)	Tennessee	1837–1865
John McKinley (1780–1852)	Alabama	1837–1852
Peter V. Daniel (1784–1860)	Virginia	1841–1860
Samuel Nelson (1792–1873)	New York	1845–1872
Levi Woodbury (1789–1851)	New Hampshire	1845–1851
Robert C. Grier (1794–1870)	Pennsylvania	1846–1870
Benjamin R. Curtis (1809–1874)	Massachusetts	1851–1857
John A. Campbell (1811–1889)	Alabama	1853–1861
Nathan Clifford (1803–1881)	Maine	1858–1881
Noah H. Swayne (1804–1884)	Ohio	1862–1881
Samuel F. Miller (1816–1890)	Iowa	1862–1890
David Davis (1815–1886)	Illinois	1862–1877
Stephen J. Field (1816–1899)	California	1863–1897
Salmon P. Chase (1808–1873)	Ohio	1864–1873
William Strong (1808–1895)	Pennsylvania	1870–1880
Joseph P. Bradley (1813–1892)	New Jersey	1870–1892
Ward Hunt (1810–1886)	New York	1873–1882
Morrison R. Waite (1816–1888)	Ohio	1874–1888
John M. Harlan (1833–1911)	Kentucky	1877–1911
William B. Woods (1824–1887)	Georgia	1881–1887
Stanley Matthews (1824–1889)	Ohio	1881–1889
Horace Gray (1828–1902)	Massachusetts	1882–1902
Samuel Blatchford (1820–1893)	New York	1882–1893
Lucius Q.C. Lamar (1825–1893)	Mississippi	1888–1893
Melville W. Fuller (1833–1910)	Illinois	1888–1910
David J. Brewer (1837–1910)	Kansas	1890–1910
Henry B. Brown (1836–1913)	Michigan	1891–1906
George Shiras, Jr. (1832–1924)	Pennsylvania	1892–**1903**
Howell E. Jackson (1832–1895)	Tennessee	1893–**1895**
Edward D. White (1845–1921)	Louisiana	1894–1910
Rufus W. Peckham (1838–1909)	New York	**1896–1909**
Joseph McKenna (1843–1926)	California	1898–**1925**
Oliver W. Holmes (1841–1935)	Massachusetts	1902–1932
William R. Day (1849–1923)	Ohio	1903–1922
William H. Moody (1853–1917)	Massachusetts	1906–1910
Horace H. Lurton (1844–1914)	Tennessee	1910–1914

Name	State	Term
Charles E. Hughes (1862–1948)	New York	1910–1916
Willis Van Devanter (1859–1941)	Wyoming	1911–1937
Joseph R. Lamar (1857–1916)	Georgia	1911–1916
Edward D. White (1845–1921)	Louisiana	1910–1921
Mahlon Pitney (1858–1924)	New Jersey	1912–1922
James C. McReynolds (1862–1946)	Tennessee	**1914–1941**
Louis D. Brandeis (1856–1941)	Massachusetts	1916–1939
John H. Clarke (1857–1945)	Ohio	1916–1922
William H. Taft (1857–1930)	Connecticut	1921–1930
George Sutherland (1862–1942)	Utah	1922–1938
Pierce Butler (1866–1939)	Minnesota	1922–1939
Edward T. Sanford (1865–1930)	Tennessee	1923–1930
Harlan F. Stone (1872–1946)	New York	**1925–1941**
Charles E. Hughes (1862–1948)	New York	1930–1941
Owen J. Roberts (1875–1955)	Pennsylvania	1930–1945
Benjamin N. Cardozo (1870–1938)	New York	**1932–1938**
Hugo L. Black (1886–1971)	Alabama	1937–1971
Stanley F. Reed (1884–	Kentucky	1938–1957
Felix Frankfurter (1882–1965)	Massachusetts	1939–1962
William O. Douglas (1898–	Connecticut	1939–
Frank Murphy (1890–1949)	Michigan	1940–1949
Harlan F. Stone (1872–1946)	New York	1941–1946
James F. Byrnes (1879–1972)	South Carolina	**1941–1942**
Robert H. Jackson (1892–1954)	New York	1941–1954
Wiley B. Rutledge (1894–1949)	Iowa	1943–1949
Harold H. Burton (1888–1964)	Ohio	1945–1958
Fred M. Vinson (1890–1953)	Kentucky	1946–1953
Tom C. Clark (1899–	Texas	1949–1967
Sherman Minton (1890–1965)	Indiana	1949–1956
Earl Warren (1891–	California	1953–1969
John Marshall Harlan (1899–1971)	New York	1955–1971
William J. Brennan, Jr. (1906–	New Jersey	1956–
Charles E. Whittaker (1901–	Missouri	1957–1962
Potter Stewart (1915–	Ohio	1958–
Byron R. White (1917–	Colorado	1962–
Arthur J. Goldberg (1908–	Illinois	1962–1965
Abe Fortas (1910–	Tennessee	1965–1969
Thurgood Marshall (1908–	New York	1967–
Warren E. Burger (1907–	Minnesota	1969–
Harry A. Blackmun (1908–	Minnesota	1970–
Lewis F. Powell, Jr. (1907–	Virginia	1972–
William H. Rehnquist (1924–	Arizona	1972–

SELECTED REFERENCES

Books designated by an asterisk (*) are available in paperback.

Abraham, Henry J. *Freedom and the Court: Civil Rights and Liberties in the United States* (1967).*

Alfange, Dean. *The Supreme Court and the National Will* (1937).

Beard, Charles A. *An Economic Interpretation of the Constitution of the United States* (rev. ed., 1935).

Beth, Loren P. *Politics, the Constitution, and the Supreme Court* (1962).*

Bickel, Alexander M. *Politics and the Warren Court* (1965).

Black, Charles L., Jr. *The People and the Court: Judicial Review in a Democracy* (1960).

Bragdon, Henry W., and Pettinger, John C. *Pursuit of Justice: An Introduction to Constitutional Rights* (1970).

Breckenridge, Adam C. *Congress against the Court* (1970).

Brown, Robert E. *Charles Beard and the Constitution* (1956).

Cahn, Edmond N., ed. *Supreme Court and Supreme Law* (1954).

Cardozo, Benjamin N. *The Nature of the Judicial Process* (1921).*

Carr, Robert K. *The Supreme Court and Judicial Review* (1942).*

Chafee, Zechariah, Jr. *Free Speech in the United States* (1941).*

Corwin, Edward S. *The Doctrine of Judicial Review* (1914).

———. *The President, Office and Powers* (4th ed., 1957).

Corwin, Edward S., and Peltason, Jack W. *Understanding the Constitution* (4th ed., 1967).

Coxe, Brinton. *Essay on Judicial Power and Unconstitutional Legislation* (1893).

Crosskey, William W. *Politics and the Constitution in the History of the United States* (2 vols., 1953).

Curtis, Charles P., Jr. *Lions under the Throne: A Study of the Supreme Court* (1947).

Cushman, Robert E., and Cushman, Robert F., eds. *Cases in Constitutional Law* (3rd ed., 1968).

Dumbauld, Edward. *The Declaration of Independence and What It Means Today* (1950).

Eidelberg, Paul. *The Philosophy of the American Constitution: A Reinterpretation of the Intentions of the Founding Fathers* (1968).*

Farrand, Max. *Framing of the Constitution of the United States* (1913).*

Frank, John P. *Marble Palace: The Supreme Court in American Life* (1968).

Freund, Paul S. *The Supreme Court of the United States: Its Business, Purposes and Performance* (1961).*

Gellhorn, Walter. *Individual Freedom and Governmental Restraints* (1956).

Hand, Learned. *The Bill of Rights* (1958).*

Hirschfield, Robert S. *The Constitution and the Court* (1962).*

Holcombe, Arthur N. *Our More Perfect Union: From Eighteenth-Century Principles to Twentieth-Century Practice* (1950).

Hyneman, Charles S. *The Supreme Court on Trial* (1963).

James, Joseph B. *The Framing of the Fourteenth Amendment* (1956).*

Jensen, Merrill. *The Articles of Confederation* (1948).

Kallenbach, Joseph E. *Federal Cooperation with the States under the Commerce Clause* (1942).

Kalven, Harry, Jr. *The Negro and the First Amendment* (1965).*

Kelly, Alfred H., and Harbison, Winfred. *The American Constitution* (4th ed., 1970).

Konefsky, Samuel J. *The Legacy of Holmes and Brandeis* (1956).

Konvitz, Milton R. *The Bill of Rights Reader* (4th ed., 1968).

Krislov, Samuel. *The Supreme Court and Political Freedom* (1968).*

Kurland, Philip B. *Politics, the Constitution and the Warren Court* (1970).

McDonald, Forrest. *We the People: The Economic Origins of the Constitution* (1958).*

McLaughlin, Andrew C. *Constitutional History of the United States* (1935).

Mason, Alpheus T. *Harlan Fiske Stone, Pillar of the Law* (1956).

———. *The Supreme Court from Taft to Warren* (rev. ed., 1969).

Mendelson, Wallace. *The Constitution and the Supreme Court* (2nd ed., 1965).

Mitau, G. Theodore. *Decade of Decision: The Supreme Court and the Constitutional Revolution 1954–1964* (1967).*

North, Arthur A. *The Supreme Court: Judicial Process and Judicial Politics* (1966).*

Palmer, Benjamin W. *Marshall and Taney, Statesmen of the Law* (1966).

Powell, Thomas Reed. *Vagaries and Varieties of Constitutional Interpretation* (1956).

Pritchett, Charles H. *The American Constitution* (2nd ed., 1968).

Pusey, Merlo J. *Charles Evans Hughes,* Vol. 2 (1951).

Read, Conyers. *The Constitution Reconsidered* (rev. ed., 1968).

Roche, John P. *Courts and Rights: The American Judiciary in Action* (2nd ed., 1966).

————. "The Founding Fathers, a Reform Caucus in Action." *American Political Science Review* 55 (1961): 799–816.

Rutland, Robert A. *Birth of the Bill of Rights, 1776–1791* (1961).*

Schmidhauser, John R. *The Supreme Court as Final Arbiter in Federal-State Relations, 1789–1957* (1958).

Schwartz, Bernard. *Reins of Power: A Constitutional History of the United States* (1963).*

Shapiro, Martin. *Freedom of Speech: the Supreme Court and Judicial Review* (1966).*

Smith, Edward C., and Zurcher, Arnold J. *Dictionary of American Politics* (2nd ed., 1968).*

Spicer, George W. *The Supreme Court and Fundamental Freedoms* (1959).*

Swisher, Carl B. *American Constitutional Development* (1954).

————. *The Supreme Court in Modern Role* (rev. ed., 1965).

Tresolini, Rocco J. *These Liberties: Case Studies in Civil Rights* (1968).*

Vile, M. J. C. *Constitutionalism and the Separation of Powers* (1967).

Warren, Charles. *The Supreme Court in United States History* (1928).

Wechsler, Herbert. *Principles, Politics and Fundamental Law* (1961).

Wright, Benjamin F. *The Growth of American Constitutional Law* (1942).*

Young, Alford. *Ratification of the Constitution* (1965).

INDEX GUIDE
TO THE CONSTITUTION

PREAMBLE

ARTICLE I
Legislative Department: organization, powers, and restraints.

ARTICLE II
Executive Department: powers, restraints, duties and election of the President.

ARTICLE III
Judicial Department: powers, restraints. Definition of treason.

ARTICLE IV
Relation of States to each other and to the Federal Government. Guarantees to States. Government of Territories.

ARTICLE V
Method of Amending Constitution. Guarantee of equal representation of States in the United States Senate.

ARTICLE VI
Provision for national debts. Supremacy of the United States Constitution, Federal laws and treaties. Pledge of national and state officials to uphold Constitution. No religious test required as qualification to public office.

ARTICLE VII
Method for ratification of the Constitution.

AMENDMENTS

The first ten amendments are called the Bill of Rights.

    I   Freedom of religion, speech, the press, and assembly.

   II   Right to keep and bear arms.

  III   Limitation on quartering of soldiers in private houses.

  IV   Limitation on searches and seizures.

   V   Protection of personal and property rights.

  VI   Right to speedy, public, and fair trial.

 VII   Trial by jury in civil cases.

VIII   Excessive bail and cruel punishments prohibited.

  IX   People possess other rights besides those enumerated.

   X   Undelegated powers belong to the States or to the people.

  XI   Exemption of States from suit by citizens of other States.

 XII   Election of President (supersedes part of Article II, sec. 1).

XIII   Slavery prohibited.

XIV   Definition of citizenship. Guarantees of due process of law and equal protection of the laws against infringement by States. Constitutional adjustments to post-Civil War conditions.

 XV   Right of adult male citizens to vote.

XVI   Congress empowered to impose an income tax.

XVII   Popular election of United States Senators.

XVIII   Prohibition of intoxicating liquors for beverage purposes.

XIX   Right of women to vote.

XX   Change in congressional and presidential terms. Abolition of the "lame duck" session of Congress.

XXI   Repeal of the Eighteenth Amendment.

XXII   Limitation of President's terms of office.

XXIII   Presidential vote for District of Columbia.

XXIV   Poll tax prohibited in election of national officers.

XXV   Vice President to become Acting President when President is unable to perform his duties.

XXVI   Suffrage extended to eighteen-year-olds in both state and national elections.

ALPHABETICAL INDEX OF CASES

Ableman v. Booth, 67
Adair v. United States, 83
Adamson v. California, 112
Adkins v. Children's Hospital, 84
Adler v. Board of Education, 102
Afroyim v. Rusk, 119
Albertson v. Subversive Activities
  Control Board, 113
American Communications Associa-
  tion v. Douds, 102
American Insurance Co. v. Canter, 87
Aptheker v. Secretary of State, 93
Argerdinger v. Hamlin, 117
Ashwander v. Tennessee Valley
  Authority, 86
Atherton v. Atherton, 69

Bailey v. Alabama, 118
Bailey v. Drexel Furniture Co., 75
Bakelite Corporation, Ex parte, 97
Baker v. Carr, 72
Barbier v. Connolly, 123
Barenblatt v. United States, 74
Barron v. Baltimore, 100
Bartkus v. Illinois, 114
Benton v. Maryland, 114
Block v. Hirsh, 86
Board of Education v. Allen, 109
Bolling v. Sharp, 125
Bond v. Floyd, 73
Book Named "John Cleland's Memoirs
  of a Woman of Pleasure
  (Fanny Hill), A," v. Attorney
  General of Massachusetts, 106
Brandenburg v. Ohio, 104
Branzburg v. Hayes, 106

Brown v. Board of Education of
  Topeka, 125
Brown v. Maryland, 80
Buchanan v. Warley, 124
Bunting v. Oregon, 122
Burstyn v. Wilson, 107

Cantwell v. Connecticut, 107
Chambers v. Florida, 111
Chaplinsky v. New Hampshire, 102
Charles River Bridge v. Warren
  Bridge, 90
Cherokee Cases, 87
Cherokee Nation v. Georgia, 87
Chisholm v. Georgia, 97
Civil Rights Cases, 123
Clark Distilling Co. v. Western
  Maryland Ry. Co., 80
Cohens v. Virginia, 98
Colegrove v. Green, 72
Coleman v. Miller, 66
Collector v. Day, 74
Communist Party of America v.
  Subversive Activities Control
  Board, 103
Cooley v. Port Wardens, 79
Cox v. Louisiana, 105
Coyle v. Smith, 68
Crandall v. Nevada, 120
Cummings v. Missouri, 89

Danbury Hatters' Case, 83
Daniel Ball, The, 78
Dartmouth College v. Woodward, 89
Debs, In re, 91
DeJonge v. Oregon, 104

DeLima v. Bidwell, 87
Dennis v. United States, 102
Downes v. Bidwell, 87
Dred Scott v. Sandford, 118
Duncan v. Louisiana, 115

Edwards v. California, 70
Edwards v. South Carolina, 105
Engel v. Vitale, 109
Erie Railroad v. Tompkins, 100
Escobedo v. Illinois, 117
Estes v. Texas, 107
Euclid v. Ambler Realty Co., 121
Evans v. Gore, 97
Everson v. Board of Education, 108

Fertilizing Company v. Hyde Park,
    120
Field v. Clark, 88
Flag Salute Cases, 108
Flast v. Cohen, 77
Fletcher v. Peck, 65
Fong Yue Ting v. United States, 94
Foster v. Neilson, 92
Frothingham v. Mellon, 76
Furman v. Georgia, 116

Garland, Ex parte, 96
Gibbons v. Ogden, 77
Gideon v. Wainwright, 117
Ginzberg v. United States, 107
Gitlow v. New York, 101
Glidden Co. v. Zdanok, 97
Gravel v. United States, 73
Graves v. New York ex rel. O'Keefe,
    76
Green v. County Board of New Kent
    County, 125
Green v. Frazier, 76
Grosjean v. American Press Co., 106
Grossman, Ex parte, 96
Grovey v. Townsend, 72
Guinn v. United States, 70

Haddock v. Haddock, 69
Hague v. C.I.O., 105
Hammer v. Dagenhart, 84
Harper v. Virginia State Board of
    Elections, 70
Harris v. New York, 117
Hawaii v. Mankichi, 88
Hawke v. Smith, 66

Head Money Cases, 93
Heart of Atlanta Motel, Inc. v.
    United States, 78
Helvering v. Davis, 77
Helvering v. Gerhardt, 75
Hepburn v. Griswold, 85
Holden v. Hardy, 121
Home Building and Loan Association
    v. Blaisdell, 90
"Hot Oil" Cases, 88
Houston E. & W. Texas Ry. Co. v.
    United States, 79
Humphrey's Executor (Rathbun) v.
    United States, 92
Huron Portland Cement Co. v. City
    of Detroit, 80
Hurtado v. California, 114

Insular Cases, 87

Johnson v. Zerbst, 117
Jones v. Alfred H. Mayer Co., 118
Juilliard v. Greenman, 85

Kansas v. Colorado, 99
Katz v. United States, 110
Kendall v. United States, 90
Kent v. Dulles, 93
Kentucky v. Dennison, 99
Keyishian v. Board of Regents, 103
Kilbourn v. Thompson, 73
Kirkpatrick v. Preiser, 73
Knowlton v. Moore, 75
Knox v. Lee, 85
Korematsu v. United States, 96

Legal Tender Cases, 85
Leisy v. Hardin, 80
Lemon v. Kurtzman, 110
Lochner v. New York, 122
Loewe v. Lawlor, 83
Louisiana ex rel. Francis v. Resweber,
    113
Luther v. Borden, 68

McCardle, Ex parte, 98
McCollom.v. Board of Education, 108
McCray v. United States, 75
McCulloch v. Maryland, 66
McGrain v. Daugherty, 72
McLaurin v. Oklahoma State Regents,
    125

Mallory v. United States, 112
Malloy v. Hogan, 112
Mapp v. Ohio, 110
Marbury v. Madison, 65
Martin v. Hunter's Lessee, 98
Martin v. Mott, 95
Massachusetts v. Mellon, 76
Maxwell v. Dow, 114
Meyer v. Nebraska, 121
Milligan, Ex parte, 95
Minersville School District v. Gobitis, 108
Miranda v. Arizona, 117
Mississippi v. Johnson, 91
Missouri ex rel. Gaines v. Canada, 124
Missouri v. Holland, 94
Morgan v. Virginia, 124
Mulford v. Smith, 83
Muller v. Oregon, 122
Munn v. Illinois, 120
Myers v. United States, 92

Nashville, Chattanooga and St. Louis Railway v. Wallace, 98
National Labor Relations Board v. Jones and Laughlin Steel Corp., 82
Neagle, In re, 91
Near v. Minnesota, 105
Nebbia v. New York, 121
Newberry v. United States, 71
New York Times Co. v. Sullivan, 106
Nixon v. Condon, 71
Nixon v. Herndon, 71
Noble State Bank v. Haskell, 120
Norman v. Baltimore and Ohio Railroad, 85
Norris v. Alabama, 115
Northern Securities Co. v. United States, 81

Ogden v. Saunders, 89
Olmstead v. United States, 110
Oregon v. Mitchell, 71

Pacific States Telephone and Telegraph Co. v. Oregon, 69
Palko v. Connecticut, 112
Panama Refining Co. v. Ryan, 88
Parker v. Davis, 85
Patton v. United States, 115

Paul v. Virginia, 82
Pennsylvania v. Nelson, 67
Pensacola Telegraph Co. v. Western Union Telegraph Co., 77
Perez v. Brownell, 119
Perry v. United States, 85
Pierce v. Society of Sisters, 107
Pipe Line Cases, 78
Plessy v. Ferguson, 123
Pollock v. Farmers' Loan and Trust Co., 74
Pollock v. Williams, 118
Powell v. Alabama, 116
Powell v. McCormick, 73
Prize Cases, The, 95

Quirin, Ex parte, 95

Reid v. Covert, 94
Reynolds v. Sims, 72
Roth v. United States, 106

Scales v. United States, 103
Schechter Poultry Co. v. United States, 81
Schenck v. United States, 101
Schneider v. Rusk, 119
School District of Abington Township v. Schempp, 109
Scott v. Sandford, 118
Scottsboro Cases, 115, 116
Selective Draft Law Cases, 81
Shelley v. Kraemer, 124
Sherrer v. Sherrer, 70
Shreveport Rate Case, 78
Siebold, Ex parte, 70
Slaughterhouse Cases, 120
Slochower v. Board of Higher Education, 112
Smith v. Allwright, 72
Social Security Cases, 77
South Carolina v. Katzenbach, 70
South Carolina v. United States, 75
South Carolina Highway Department v. Barnwell Bros., 79
Southern Pacific Co. v. Arizona, 79
Standard Oil Co. v. United States, 81
Stearns v. Minnesota, 68
Steward Machine Co. v. Davis, 77
Strauder v. West Virginia, 114
Stromberg v. California, 104
Swann v. Charlotte-Mecklenburg County Board of Education, 126

Sweatt v. Painter, 125
Swift v. Tyson, 100
Swift & Co. v. United States, 81

Terry v. Adams, 72
Terry v. Ohio, 111
Texas Primary Cases, 71
Texas v. White, 68
Thornhill v. Alabama, 104
Tilton v. Richardson, 110
Toth v. Quarles, 96
Trop v. Dulles, 116
Truax v. Raich, 124
Twining v. New Jersey, 111
Tyson v. Banton, 121

Ullmann v. United States, 112
United States v. Appalachian Power
    Co., 78
United States v. Belmont, 94
United States v. Brown, 89
United States v. Butler, 76
United States v. Classic, 71
United States v. Curtiss-Wright Export
    Corporation, 88, 93
United States v. Darby, 84
United States v. E. C. Knight Co., 81
United States v. Interstate Commerce
    Commission, 82
United States v. Jackson, 115
United States v. Lovett, 89
United States v. O'Brien, 104
United States v. Peters, 67
United States v. South-Eastern Under-
    writers Association, 82
United States v. United States District

Court for the Eastern District
    of Michigan, 111
United States v. Wong Kim Ark, 119

Veazie Bank v. Fenno, 84
Virginia v. West Virginia, 99

Wabash, St. Louis, and Pacific R.R.
    Co. v. Illinois, 78
Walz v. Tax Commission of the City
    of New York, 109
Watkins v. United States, 74
Wesberry v. Sanders, 72
West Coast Hotel Co. v. Parrish, 122
West Virginia State Board of Edu-
    cation v. Barnette, 108
Whitney v. California, 101
Wickard v. Filburn, 83
Wiener v. United States, 92
Williams v. North Carolina, 69
Wilson v. New, 83
Wisconsin Rate Case, 79
Witherspoon v. Illinois, 115
Wolff Packing Co. v. Court of
    Industrial Relations, 122
Woods v. Miller, 86
Worcester v. Georgia, 87

Yakus v. United States, 88
Yates v. United States, 103
Yick Wo v. Hopkins, 123
Youngstown Sheet and Tube Co. v.
    Sawyer, 91

Zicarelli v. New Jersey State Com-
    mittee of Investigation, 113
Zorach v. Clauson, 108